An Advent

An exploration of the
for the weekday

Michael T Winstanley SDB

Credits

Scripture Quotations

Artwork by Val O'Brien

Cover Photo by Michael T Winstanley

Back Cover Picture
Nativity by Pieter de Grebber
Manchester City Galleries

Published by
Don Bosco Publications
Thornleigh House
Sharples Park
BOLTON BL1 6PQ
www.don-bosco-publications.co.uk
sarah@salesians.org.uk
© 2014
ISBN 978-1-909080-12-6

Fonts used
Main Text – Calibri
Scripture – Bookman Old Style
Headings – Bookman Old Style
Endnotes – Palatino Roman

Endnotes are provided at the end of each chapter for reference and as suggestions for further reading. They will prove invaluable for a deeper appreciation of the scriptural text.

Printed by
Buxton Press Limited
Palace Road, Buxton, Derbyshire, SK17 6AE

Contents

Introduction

We are about to set out on our Advent journey. Advent, I maintain, is such a beautiful liturgical season, one in which I always feel at home and which I enjoy. The basic meaning of the word, as we know so well, is *coming* or *arrival*. So Advent is a period of waiting for someone to come, for the *coming of the Lord*. It's a time of anticipation and preparation.

We all know what it is like to wait. It is a common aspect of our daily lives, a factor which, for many of us, seems to be on the increase. We wait at the traffic lights or roadworks. We get snarled up in a jam on the motorway or in our local town at peak times. We wait for loved ones or colleagues at airports and railway stations, frequently consulting information screens and our watch, or texting. We wait for the post to arrive, for people to answer our letters and enquiries, or to respond to emails. We wait for someone to answer the phone as we are transferred from one extension to another. We wait for appointments or results at the medical centre or hospital. We wait for service in shops and cafes. We wait for the birth of a child in our family, or for someone to die. Elsewhere in our world, people are waiting for a war to cease, for food to be brought in, for a well to be dug, for markets to open for their produce. Waiting provokes a wide range of emotions. We can be frustrated, impatient or angry. We can become anxious as we wait, even fearful, excited or hopeful. Much depends, obviously, on what or whom we are waiting for. Waiting, I think, always increases our awareness that we are not in control, that we can't always change things, that we can't dictate the pace and determine the outcome, that we are dependent, that we are *poor*. Because of this, waiting has enormous potential for growth in Christian discipleship.

In Advent we seem to be waiting at three levels. Firstly, and this occurs particularly through the readings from the Old Testament at Mass, we are caught up in the longing, hoping and waiting of the people of Israel for the coming of the Messiah, the person whom God would send to bring them forgiveness and freedom, peace, joy and prosperity. We live with them the unfolding of their dreams as, through the great prophets, they articulate their yearnings. We find that many of those yearnings and dreams strike chords in our own hearts, for they are also the basic yearnings and needs of humankind. As we read and ponder, we are drawn into their hopes, their trust in God's faithful love, their assurance that God will be true to the promises made. We can also identify with their strong awareness of their need to be saved; we share their poverty of being, their humble dependence.

Secondly, as Christian believers we know that this Old Testament waiting and anticipation was historically fulfilled in the actual coming of Jesus: his birth in Bethlehem, his life among us, culminating in his brutal death, his resurrection and the outpouring of his Spirit. So there is for us a looking back, a remembering in wonder and thanksgiving. But there is also a looking forward. We are awaiting, anticipating and preparing for our liturgical celebration of that coming and all that it means – preparing for Christmas. Caught up in the event as a present reality, we believe that in our liturgy that past moment is made present again. Jesus will be savingly present among us again on December 25th. Christmas is a graced moment, a particularly strong and gentle experience of God's presence in our midst, his being *with us,* our Emmanuel, as Matthew would say. Liturgy is a re-presentation, a making present again. We feel the excitement associated with the coming of a very dear friend. There is the external preparation in its many dimensions, and the preparation of our hearts for that coming. This is a very special waiting.

In the third place, our looking to the past whilst celebrating in the present also points us to the future again, but this time from our current perspective. In many of the Advent readings, especially on Sundays, there is a sense of waiting, anticipating, preparing for that other coming of Jesus the Lord at the end: at the end of life, at the end of the world.

The latter is sometimes referred to as *the second coming* or *parousia*. There is a different feel about this kind of waiting that is linked with the element of his coming in judgement as well as his coming for salvation. For us, as adults, our Advent celebration points us in the direction of the total experience of God's presence in loving faithfulness in some future time. This dimension perhaps helps us keep the other dimensions in perspective. But there is continuity. The best way to prepare for the second coming is to prepare well for Christmas, and allow that coming of Jesus to transform our hearts and our lives. Even if we aren't quite as youthful as we used to be, there is still a magic in the three levels of the Advent season.

In this book I propose to examine and reflect upon the Gospel readings for the weekdays of Advent as one way of focusing our waiting and our preparing for Christmas. Most of the readings for the first three weeks are taken from Matthew's Gospel, with a few from Luke's and one from John's.[1] Mark's Gospel fails to feature at all, unfortunately. For the final eight days the excerpts are taken from the Infancy Narratives of Matthew and Luke respectively. I have given the book the title *An Advent Journey*. The Infancy Narratives describe several journeys; during his subsequent ministry Jesus seems almost always to be on the move. Luke particularly stresses this journey motif, using it as the framework for exploring aspects of discipleship.[2] I like to view Advent as a time of journeying towards the celebration of Christmas, with the stopping and starting that is typical of every journey, and with the struggle and anticipation which many journeys regularly entail. I have included a final chapter called *Journey's End*, in which I address the Gospel readings for the three Masses of Christmas Day.

For each passage considered during the four week journey I have used the same approach and format that I have adopted elsewhere.[3] In the first place I try to locate the extract in its wider Gospel context, and then make relevant exegetical comments in order to explore and clarify the content of the episode. My main preoccupation is to highlight the theological message of each passage: the word from God. But God's word is conveyed through human language, and I sometimes refer to significant literary features of the text.[4] Occasionally, historical issues arise and must be addressed.[5] Secondly, I offer some brief personal reflections arising from the text, which I hope will be helpful to the reader as a stimulus for prayer and pondering. The English version which I use is the NRSV, which I believe renders the original Greek most faithfully.[6]

The written Gospels were the outcome of a complex process of development beginning from the initial impact which Jesus made on his followers during his ministry, this became the core of the apostolic testimony and preaching. This Jesus tradition, the remembering of what Jesus said and did, was handed on orally in a world which was largely illiterate. In such community oral transmission, there is inevitably variation, but since its purpose is primarily to recall and preserve what is valued from the past, the nucleus or core content tends to remain stable and fixed.[7] In the light of the resurrection and the subsequent outpouring of the Holy Spirit, deeper dimensions of the historical ministry and death of Jesus came to be appreciated, this new understanding was reflected in the telling of the story of Jesus. Development occurred over a period of some forty to seventy years, as the early Christian communities grew and spread and reacted to their own changing environment and to the various challenges which faced them, from within and without. Liturgy, worship and catechetical instruction exerted a significant influence. Eventually, from a variety of traditions about the teaching and life of Jesus which were circulating in many communities of faith, Mark composed the first written Gospel; through originality, technical skills and theological acumen, he created a connected narrative.[8] For the ministry of Jesus, Matthew and Luke drew on Mark, their own special sources and oral traditions, and a further written source, no longer extant, known as Q, containing many of Jesus' sayings.[9] Their Infancy Narratives are derived from their own sources and creativity; in many respects they are very different from each other, but there are significant similarities.[10]

John's Gospel was written independently of the others, and has its own very distinctive style, symbolism and theology. Occasionally, there are clear points of contact with similar early traditions.[11]

The Gospels are a wonderful weaving together of history and theology, as they report the events of Christ's life intertwined with later understandings of Christ from the communities of the first century.[12]

In presenting this book I acknowledge my enormous debt to the writings of numerous scholars which I have consulted over the years. Their learning, insights and integrity have been instructive and inspirational. I have tried to write in a non-technical style, hoping that this book will be accessible to a wide readership, lay, religious and clergy of all denominations, who wish to deepen their understanding of Jesus and his message, and to explore the implications of discipleship for today. It can be used for personal study, prayer and reflection. It can also be used for Christian groups of various kinds: prayer groups, bible study groups, retreatants, teachers, catechists and students at different levels.

I wish to thank Fr Tony Bailey SDB and the staff of Don Bosco Publications for their patience and expertise in preparing the manuscript for publication, and Fr Kieran Anderson SDB, who read the text and made useful suggestions. Finally, I thank my Salesian confreres and many other friends, contemporary disciples of Jesus, for their encouragement, inspiration and support over many years. I have dedicated this book to Fr Bernard Higgins SDB, recently deceased, who as Salesian Provincial many years ago asked me to join the teaching staff and the Salesian community at Ushaw College, Durham, a decision which gave me the opportunity to study and teach the Gospels. May he enjoy the fullness of life in God's loving presence.

Michael T Winstanley SDB

Bolton, June 2014.

Endnotes

1. 12 from Matthew, 4 from Luke, 1 from John.
2. Luke 9:51-19:27; for more details see Tuesday of Week One.
3. See M.T. Winstanley, *Lenten Sundays* (Bolton, Don Bosco Publications 2011).
4. This area of study (form, source and redaction criticism) is fascinating; though literary, it is also strongly historical. See J.R. Donahue & D. Harrington, *The Gospel of Mark* (Collegeville, Liturgical Press 2002), p.1-22. A development, of the last 25 years or so, is the study of the Gospels as story; it is called narrative criticism. See D. Rhoads and D. Michie, *Mark as Story* (Philadelphia, Fortress 1982); M.A. Powell, *What is Narrative Criticism?* (Minneapolis, Fortress 1990); J.L. Ressaguie, *Narrative Criticism of the New Testament. An Introduction* (Grand Rapids, Baker Academic 2005).
5. There are, for instance, a number of important historical issues in the Infancy Narratives.
6. The NRSV is based on *The Greek New Testament* (United Bible Societies 1983).
7. See the treatment of these issues in J.D.G. Dunn, *A New Perspective,* (London, SPCK 2005), p.46-56, and R.K. McIver, *Memory, Jesus and the Synoptic Gospels* (Resources for Biblical Study 59; Atlanta, SBL 2011); his conclusions are found on p.183-187.
8. B. Byrne, *A Costly Freedom* (Collegeville, Liturgical Press 2008), p.xvi, xx. This is not to deny that before Mark the oral tradition had already developed narrative or kerygmatic blocks or sequences; see Dunn, *A New Perspective,* p.124. Mark probably wrote soon after AD 70, the year of the destruction of Jerusalem by the Romans. A long tradition maintains that he wrote in Rome, and a majority of scholars still accept this view. Others suggest a place closer to Palestine, like southern Syria. Most commentaries on Mark deal with these issues in some detail.

9. This is the commonly accepted scholarly opinion. 'Q' comes from the German *Quelle* meaning a source. It is possible that there were different versions of 'Q'. Matthew and Luke probably wrote in the mid-eighties.

10. See R.E. Brown, *The Birth of the Messiah* (London, Chapman 1993), p.34-37; J.A. Fitzmyer, *The Gospel according to Luke I-IX* (New York, Doubleday 1981), p.306-309; P.A. McDonald, *Resemblances between Matthew 1-2 and Luke 1-2* in *New Perspectives on the Nativity*, ed. J.Corley (London, T&T Clark 2009), p.200-201.

11. There is much discussion about the authorship of the Fourth Gospel. The long tradition which identifies three figures: John the son of Zebedee, the Beloved Disciple and the Gospel's author, is no longer generally held to be accurate. Today some scholars believe that a minor disciple during Jesus' ministry (later known as the Beloved Disciple) had an important role in the founding of the Johannine community and was the source of its tradition about Jesus. This tradition developed through decades of reflection, liturgical celebration, struggles and lived experience, and was eventually fashioned into our Gospel, probably at Ephesus, between AD 90-100 by an unknown but very gifted member of the community, himself a disciple of the Beloved Disciple. Another member of the community (usually referred to as *the redactor*) revised the text shortly afterwards, making a few additions. See R.E. Brown, *An Introduction to the New Testament* (New York, Doubleday 1997), p.368-371; R.A. Culpepper, *The Gospel and Letters of John* (Nashville, Abingdon Press 1998), p.29-41. For a recent study of the relationship between the Gospels, see P.N. Anderson, *The Riddles of the Fourth Gospel. An Introduction to John* (Minneapolis, Fortress 2011).

12. The Catholic Bishops' Conference of England and Wales, *The Gift of Scripture*, (London, CTS 2005), p.35. See also C.R. Koester, *The Word of Life* (Grand Rapids, Eerdmans 2008), p.7; J.D.G. Dunn, *Jesus Remembered* (Cambridge, Eerdmans 2003); R. Bauckham, *Jesus and the Eyewitnesses* (Grand Rapids, Eerdmans 2006); R.K. McKiver, *Memory*.

Week One

Monday - Week One

The Centurion in Matthew

Astory about Jesus healing a centurion's servant occurs quite early in the Gospels of Matthew and Luke.[1] In Luke's version the centurion sends some of the village elders to intercede with Jesus. They are willing to do this on the grounds that he is friendly towards the Jews of the town. In Matthew it is the centurion himself who personally approaches him with his request.[2] It is this encounter which we shall consider in this first Advent reading. The episode is located in the block of material to be found between the Sermon on the Mount and the missionary discourse.[3] Here, Matthew picks up the Markan narrative, but thoroughly reorders and streamlines his material, and inserts two episodes not included there.[4] After his ministry of the word in the great sermon, Jesus, the messianic teacher, now exercises a messianic ministry of healing and reconciling.[5] In both words and works, which are complementary, Jesus shows great authority.[6] There are nine stories, grouped in clusters of three.[7] The encounter between Jesus and the centurion is located between the cure of the leper and the healing of Simon's mother-in-law; all three individuals were disadvantaged and for different reasons found themselves on the margins of the Jewish community.

When he entered Capernaum, a centurion came to him, appealing to him and saying, *Lord, my servant is lying at home paralysed, in terrible distress.* And he said to him, *I will come and cure him.* The centurion answered, *Lord, I am not worthy to have you come under my roof; but only speak the word, and my servant will be healed. For I also am a man under authority, with soldiers under me; and I say to one, "Go", and he goes, and to another, "Come", and he comes, and to my slave, "Do this", and the slave does it.*

12

When Jesus heard him, he was amazed and said to those who followed him, *Truly I tell you, in no one in Israel have I found such faith. I tell you, many will come from east and west and will eat with Abraham and Isaac and Jacob in the kingdom of heaven, while the heirs of the kingdom will be thrown into the outer darkness, where there will be weeping and gnashing of teeth.* And to the centurion Jesus said, *Go; let it be done for you according to your faith.* And the servant was healed in that hour. (Matt 8:5-13)

The Centurion's Approach

The setting is the frontier town of Capernaum, which Jesus seems to have made his base early in his ministry. On arriving back there, Jesus is met by a centurion from the military garrison which was manned by soldiers in the service of Herod Antipas.[8] He probably hails from Syria, and is a Gentile. Aware of Jesus' reputation, and addressing Jesus as Lord, he outlines his problem and concern, explaining that his servant is lying paralysed at home in considerable distress.[9] The response of Jesus to this approach can be taken in two ways. Usually, it is understood as a statement: *I will come and cure him.* Jesus responds immediately, even expressing his willingness to come to the centurion's house in order to bring the servant healing and relief. He is prepared to have dealings with a Gentile and even enter his home, thus incurring ritual uncleanness and, inevitably, some local displeasure.[10] The centurion is clearly dismayed by this unexpected offer which exceeds his original request, and, again addressing Jesus as Lord, acknowledges his unworthiness, particularly as a Gentile, to welcome him under his roof. He recognises the authority of Jesus, going on to voice his conviction that a word from Jesus, without making the short journey, will be sufficient to effect a cure. For, in his position and with his army experience, the centurion knows what authority is all about, and is well acquainted with the power of a word of command. If he can command with a word, all the more so can Jesus.[11]

An alternative view understands Jesus' words as an ironic question, constituting an initial hesitation or rebuff, as in the later episode of the Syro-Phoenician woman. In effect Jesus, surprised at the request, is asking, *Am I supposed to come and heal him?* – and this in a Gentile house, thus breaking the rules on purity. Scholars who are of this mind maintain that such reluctance is consistent with Jesus' later response to the woman. The centurion is aware of his unworthiness, and openly acknowledges it; he is not expecting a personal visit to his house; he is conversant with Jewish rules about ritual cleanness; he respects Jesus' authority, which renders such a visit unnecessary; he clarifies his request, offering Jesus an alternative course of action.[12]

The Response of Jesus

On hearing this reply, Jesus is amazed, and observes emphatically to those with him that he has not found insight and faith of such quality amongst the people of Israel. This is the only occasion when Matthew uses this term of Jesus.[13] The man has shown some awareness of Jesus' closeness to God. He has also sensed that as a Gentile he is not entirely excluded from Jesus' care. Jesus then authoritatively makes a telling statement.[14] Looking ahead into the future, and echoing the vision of the prophets of old, Jesus then claims that there will be many Gentiles, people from east and west, who will come to share the messianic banquet of the heavenly Kingdom with the great patriarchs Abraham, Isaac and Jacob, whilst their true natural heirs will be cast out.[15] The centurion, like the earlier Magi in Matthew's story, is the forerunner of these.[16]

In the opening verse of his Gospel, Matthew presents Jesus as Son of Abraham. Abraham is the father of the Jewish people, but also the one in whom all the nations of the world would be blessed. In 4:15, as Jesus inaugurates his ministry, making his home by the lake in Capernaum, Isaiah's reference to Galilee of the nations is recalled. Later in the narrative, Matthew quotes Isaiah concerning the Spirit-filled Servant *who will proclaim justice to the Gentiles... And in his name the Gentiles will hope.*[17]

In his final discourse Jesus predicts the preaching of the Gospel to all the nations.[18] Finally, the focusing of his ministry on the Jews, the lost sheep of the house of Israel, as expressed in his dialogue with the Syro-Phoenician woman, is superseded after his death and resurrection.[19] Back in Galilee the Risen Lord gathers his disciples, scattered by the striking down of the shepherd. He makes to them his final statement: *All authority in heaven and on earth has been given to me. Go therefore and make disciples of all nations.*[20] With the dawning of the new age, the blessings of the Kingdom are made available to all.

Jesus' words concerning the future also constitute a severe warning or threat for his Jewish listeners, who are in danger of missing the opportunity to embrace their destiny. A warning is also sounded for Matthew's Church in a different and later context; the community must not be complacent; they must continue vigorously to believe.[21]

The story itself concludes with Jesus telling the centurion to return home with the assurance that, in accordance with his faith, his request will be granted. In fact, the servant is healed that very moment, and healed at a distance. The power or sovereign authority of Jesus' word is evident, but the emphasis in the story is probably more on the centurion's faith than on the miracle.[22] *Although Jesus has come only for the lost sheep of Israel, the restriction is overcome when he meets genuine belief. Faith conquers the separation between Jew and Gentile.*[23] Perhaps the healing at a distance is intended to reflect the restriction of Jesus' ministry to Israel; maybe it is a spatial metaphor symbolising the historical fact that Gentile participation in the blessings of the Gospel is separated in time from the earthly ministry of Jesus.[24]

Reflections

This episode in Jesus' ministry provides an excellent opening for the season of Advent. The Jesus whom we meet here is welcoming and brings healing. The centurion shows great trust. This combination is compelling and paradigmatic.

Following the traditional interpretation of the story, Jesus is clearly a man of authority. He is probably surprised at being approached for a cure by a Gentile. Unusual as this is, and contrary to the normal thrust of his ministry, he responds with great openness, even spontaneously volunteering to go to the centurion's home in order to cure his servant. Clearly, such a visit was not part of the petitioner's scenario. Jesus is prepared to incur ritual defilement in order to effect the healing, and does not baulk at the probability of incurring criticism and hostility from the townsfolk for his trouble. There is a remarkable freedom and openness about him. He publically expresses his amazement at the man's extraordinary faith. Adopting the alternative interpretation of the story, Jesus manifests his flexibility, his willingness to change his attitude when faced with strong faith. He generously acknowledges in public the faith he has encountered. It is the centurion's faith which stands out from the narrative. He clearly believes in the power of Jesus to heal his servant; he trusts that his Gentile background will not prove an insurmountable obstacle. He is aware of his poverty and need. He shows humility in readily acknowledging his unworthiness to have Jesus under his roof. For him, a word from Jesus is enough.

In commenting so favourably on the Gentile's faith, Jesus puts him forward as an exemplar. This is the case not only for the Jews of the town in which the encounter took place; it is true for us today. This is perhaps particularly so as we enter the season of Advent. There is something engaging and attractive about the man's humble awareness that he has no rights and cannot demand a cure for his servant. Such poverty of spirit must be a characteristic when we approach Jesus with our hopes, dreams and needs. The man's words, slightly adapted, have been included in the new form of our Eucharistic celebration prior to the reception of communion. *Lord, I am not worthy that you should enter under my roof, but only say the word and my soul shall be healed.*[25] They sum up the dispositions which are appropriate for our welcoming of the Lord into our hearts. They also express our trust in the love and acceptance of Jesus, and his power to heal and bring life to the whole of our being. They could be our Advent prayer mantra.

The Prayer of Jesus

The Gospel extract for today is taken from Luke.[26] Its context is the early part of the lengthy central section of Luke's narrative that is usually referred to as *the journey to Jerusalem* or *the travel narrative*. The evangelist uses this journey motif from 9:51-19:27 as a kind of framework within which he can explore salient aspects of discipleship, the way of Jesus.[27] Throughout this major block of material, mainly devoted to the teaching of Jesus, there are many clear reminders of the journey theme.[28]

As the journey gets under way, Jesus sends messengers ahead of him. They go to a Samaritan village to prepare for his coming, but the villagers are not interested in receiving him because he is going up to Jerusalem. This reflects the prejudice and animosity which existed between Samaritans and Jews. James and John wish to respond in kind, and ask Jesus whether they should call down fire from heaven to burn them up, a suggestion which incurs a rebuke from the Master. As they journey on, there are three brief encounters which highlight the radical demands of discipleship. After this, the Lord appoints seventy two disciples and sends them on mission to the places he is to visit on his journey. Jesus speaks with some sadness and in tones of warning about the lakeside towns for their lack of response. The seventy two then return from their mission. They are delighted with what they have been able to do in Jesus' name. He states that they should rejoice rather that their names are written in heaven.

At that same hour Jesus rejoiced in the Holy Spirit and said, *I thank you, Father, Lord of heaven and earth, because you have hidden these things from the wise and the intelligent and have revealed them to infants; yes, Father, for such was your gracious will.*

17

All things have been handed over to me by my Father; and no one knows who the Son is except the Father, or who the Father is except the Son and anyone to whom the Son chooses to reveal him.

Then turning to the disciples, Jesus said to them privately, *Blessed are the eyes that see what you see! For I tell you that many prophets and kings desired to see what you see, but did not see it, and to hear what you hear, but did not hear it.*

(Luke 10:21-24)

The joy from the previous episode concerning mission, to which this section is closely tied, spills over, as Jesus immediately bursts into joyful prayer. He does so under the inspiration or influence of the Spirit, whose anointing had been such a significant aspect at his baptism, and in whose name he had launched his mission in the Nazareth synagogue.[29] Already Luke has several times referred to the prayer of Jesus: Jesus prays at the baptism, withdraws on occasion to quiet places, prays before the call of the Twelve, before Peter's profession of faith, and at the transfiguration.[30] Shortly after the episode we are considering, stimulated by the sight of him at prayer, the disciples will ask to be taught how to pray, and Jesus will give them their own special prayer.[31]

This time Luke does not simply state that Jesus prays, but provides the reader with the content of his prayer. The language is poetic, has a strong Semitic ring, and follows the pattern of synagogue prayers of praise and thanksgiving.[32] Jesus addresses God both as *Father* and *Lord of heaven and earth*, a form of address which at the same time acknowledges God's transcendence and otherness, and also his closeness, care and intimacy.[33] *Father* occurs here five times. Jesus thanks this God for choosing both to conceal and to reveal.[34] The message of the Kingdom's presence, revealed by the words and works of Jesus, has been hidden from the wise and intelligent religious specialists,[35] but has been made known to ordinary people, the little ones. Jesus recognises that this is God's good pleasure, God's way, which subverts traditional Jewish religious thinking.

God's predilection for the poor and lowly and needy, God's paradoxical tendency to overturn normal human values, expectations and priorities, is a theme which Luke highlights throughout his Gospel. Mary celebrates this reversal motif in the Magnificat, and from the outset of his ministry Jesus has set out to bring the Good News to the poor.[36]

Jesus moves on to reveal the relationship which stands at the basis of his prayer. Speaking in language which has a distinctly Johannine ring,[37] he shares his awareness of his unique identity and his role, his relationship with the Father as Son. The sovereign Father has gifted him with authority.[38] He is uniquely known in the depth of his being by the Father, and he knows the Father as no other does. The relationship is reciprocal. And so he alone is able to reveal the Father, and does so to those whom he chooses.[39]

Jesus next addresses the chosen disciples privately, proclaiming them blessed and happy because of what they can hear and see.[40] For they, ordinary and lowly as they are, are privileged to be living in a special time, the time of revelation, the time longed for over centuries by the prophets and kings of old, the most religious and powerful people of the ages. They are witnessing now the fulfilment of Israel's dreams in the presence and ministry of Jesus; God's Kingdom is manifest wherever Jesus is present.[41] They have been able to recognise and appreciate this also through their recent participation in his mission.

Reflections

Advent is a time of joyful rejoicing. But this rejoicing is not of the kind so frequently encountered at this time of year – the pre-Christmas *office get-together*, or its equivalents. There is, of course, a place for that. But Advent's joy stems from the realisation of what Christmas is all about, and from the keen awareness that we have been so remarkably blessed. For we know that what the prophets of old longed for and dreamed about, longings and dreams articulated in many of the Advent liturgical readings, have been fulfilled in Jesus. In a very true and profound sense, our eyes have seen and our ears have heard.

We have come to share something of the experience of Jesus' early disciples as they listened to his words and witnessed what he was doing. For all our ordinariness and weakness and mistakes, we are aware of the revelation of God's saving love, God's compassion and faithfulness.

In his prayer as recorded by Luke, Jesus addresses God as *Abba, Father*. Drawn into this intimate relationship, we too can adopt this way of speaking to God as his beloved sons and daughters. There is a wonderful familiarity about our prayer. Jesus also in his prayer acknowledges the otherness of God, who is Lord of heaven and earth, the God *beyond all names*. And it is important for us to maintain this dimension too. Like Moses at the burning bush, realising that we tread on holy ground, we take off our sandals.[42] There is respect and deep reverence in the presence of the *Other*. Familiarity and reverence are the two wings of our relationship with our God, two ongoing aspects of our prayer.

The Compassion of Jesus

The prophets of Israel are dreamers; they articulate the longings of their people for a better future; they express the hopes of most human beings through the ages for transformation. One of their favourite symbols is that of a banquet in which the food will be abundant and the wine will flow freely.[43] Another significant symbol is the mountain. Mountains rising into the skies seem nearer to heaven, and are places of God's revelations.[44] In messianic expectation, Mount Zion would be a gathering place for Israel in the end time; in that time there would be a great banquet.[45] Another key aspect of prophetic dreaming is the removing of the tears and sadness of death, and the healing of the suffering which leads up to it. Isaiah, in the first reading for today, expresses all this with great sensitivity, as he hopes deeply for the coming of the Lord to save his people.[46]

The writers of the New Testament see these hopes and longings fulfilled in Jesus. Today's Gospel extract from Matthew is a beautiful illustration of this.

After Jesus had left that place, he passed along the Sea of Galilee, and he went up the mountain, where he sat down. Great crowds came to him, bringing with them the lame, the maimed, the blind, the mute, and many others. They put them at his feet, and he cured them, so that the crowd was amazed when they saw the mute speaking, the maimed whole, the lame walking, and the blind seeing. And they praised the God of Israel.

Then Jesus called his disciples to him and said, *I have compassion for the crowd, because they have been with me now for three days and have nothing to eat; and I do not want to send them away hungry, for they might faint on the way.* The disciples said to him, *Where are we to get enough bread in the desert to feed so great a crowd?*

Jesus asked them, *How many loaves have you?* They said, *Seven, and a few small fish.* Then ordering the crowd to sit down on the ground, he took the seven loaves and the fish; and after giving thanks he broke them and gave them to the disciples, and the disciples gave them to the crowds. And all of them ate and were filled; and they took up the broken pieces left over, seven baskets full. (Matt 15:29-37)

Jesus has recently made a journey to the district of Tyre and Sidon, and spent some time there. Tyre was an ancient Phoenician cosmopolitan city mentioned in the Old Testament.[47] It still flourished as an important urban seaport, and its territory bordered on Upper Galilee; the inhabitants were not friendly towards the Jewish minority; they were an economically dominant and oppressive group.[48] There, a Canaanite woman approaches him, seeking healing for her possessed daughter. It was not appropriate for her to come to Jesus in public. She addresses him as Son of David, seeming to claim the rights of Israel. Her persistence leads the disciples to urge Jesus to send her away. He categorically states: *I was sent only to the lost sheep of the house of Israel.* She comes up closer and kneels before him, begging him to help her. Accepting that the children must eat first, she suggests that there may be crumbs for her from the Master's table. Impressed by her faith, Jesus accedes to her request. Just as she comes to see her place in God's overall design, Jesus comes to acknowledge that the Shepherd of Israel is also for all nations.[49]

On leaving the place, Jesus returns to home territory beside the familiar Sea of Galilee and heads for the hills nearby, where he sits down. For this evangelist, mountains are such an important setting.[50] There, great crowds seek him out, bringing to him the maimed, the lame, the blind, the mute and many others in need of healing.[51] Jesus cures them all in a display of extraordinary compassion, and the scene becomes a kind of verbal icon which proclaims the messianic authority of Jesus expressed in his mission of healing.[52] *With crowds of this size, Jesus' compassion is breathtaking in its scope.*[53]

The people praise the God of Israel (*For the hand of the Lord will rest on this mountain*), who is faithfully present in the ministry of Jesus.[54] This is the climax of Jesus' ministry in Galilee.

At this point the focus of Jesus' attention switches from healing the people to providing nourishment for them. The language here is very similar to the parallel passage in Mark.[55] Jesus himself acknowledges his deep compassion. It is this which drives him to respond to the hungry crowds, shepherd-like, providing them with nourishment. Jesus cares deeply about their welfare.[56] He wishes to prevent any harm coming to them on their journey home. The disciples, practical and realistic fellows, voice their awareness of the difficulty involved, the impossibility for them to provide food for so many in that place. Undeterred, Jesus instructs the crowds to sit down on the ground. He then gives thanks to God, and with the available seven loaves and a few small fish Jesus provides a banquet for the crowd, which numbers 4000 men, along with women and children.[57] All of them have as much as they wish to eat and there are abundant leftovers. The dreams of Israel are coming true in Jesus; the eschatological banquet is under way; the new age has begun.[58]

In his actions, stimulated by his compassion, Jesus is bringing the old prophecies to fulfilment. Whereas the religious leaders do nothing for the people, and the disciples wish to send them away, Jesus is open to them and caring towards them. In this he shows himself to be the compassionate, therapeutic Son of David, the eschatological Shepherd of Israel,[59] and provides an answer to the question which the Baptist voiced earlier: *Are you the one who is to come, or are we to wait for another.*[60]

Reflections

We too have dreams: dreams for healing and wholeness, dreams for nourishment and growth, dreams for change and for life. As we speak of these dreams to Jesus in prayer, he reaches out to us in compassion. Jesus was known, experienced and remembered as a man of great compassion. He hasn't changed!

One special, privileged point of encounter with him is the Eucharist. His taking the bread, giving thanks, breaking the bread and handing it over for consumption, would remind Matthew's readers of their Eucharistic celebrations.[61] The description of these gestures draws us into our celebration years later. Let us try to avoid the danger of routine, and to capture the magic of this moment. But we also need to realise that liturgical celebration is inadequate if we don't reach out in daily life to bring healing and help to the hungry and those in need.[62]

The style, outlook and message of Jesus was quite revolutionary, when you think of it. In this he was truly prophetic. He presented a different understanding of God, an alternative pattern for relating to one another, the sketch or outline of a different world. As disciples of Jesus, you and I are called to be women and men of compassion. We are called to mirror to others the compassionate God whom Jesus reveals. I've recently heard it said that our country seems to be becoming a harder, individualistic, less caring place to be, and that maybe our Church has caught the disease too. Jesus shows us a different way to think and to live. I believe it is the only way to change society. As disciples of Jesus, we are called to be prophets of compassion. We begin in our own families and communities, our neighbourhoods and places of work or recreation. Here we seek to reflect to one another the compassionate face of Jesus, the faithfulness and tender love of God. In the various aspects of our Christian ministry we seek to make compassion central.

On Wisdom and Foolishness

The prophetic imagery in today's first reading is architectural; it suggests strength, security, durability; it speaks of walls, ramparts, citadels. Whatever the surrounding architecture, however, it is the Lord who is, for his people, the everlasting, immovable, solid rock, and the source of security and peace. It is the symbol of the rock which links our two readings.

> Not everyone who says to me, *Lord, Lord,* will enter the kingdom of heaven, but only one who does the will of my Father in heaven.

> Everyone then who hears these words of mine and acts on them will be like a wise man who built his house on rock. The rain fell, the floods came, and the winds blew and beat on that house, but it did not fall, because it had been founded on rock. And everyone who hears these words of mine and does not act on them will be like a foolish man who built his house on sand. The rain fell, and the floods came, and the winds blew and beat against that house, and it fell – and great was its fall!

> (Matt 7:21, 24-27)

The extract chosen for the Gospel reading is taken from the final part of the Sermon on the Mount – that carefully constructed collection of Jesus' sayings. In this concluding section, after comments about the two gates, the two ways, and the two trees, Jesus, with exquisitely balanced symmetry, uses the imagery of two building methods and the contrasting results.[63] The powerful parable unfolds in a threefold parallel: how the house was built, the raging of the storm, and the impact or result. Jesus is highlighting contrasting discipleship styles and stressing the vital importance of the way we live.[64]

25

Jesus distinguishes between hearing and doing, and draws the distinction between the wise and the foolish.[65] Yes, it is necessary to be people of prayer, to be people who listen and reflect, but authentic discipleship demands action as well; the key verb throughout this section of the sermon is the verb *to do*. Carrying out the will of the heavenly Father is more important. Or, equivalently, acting in accordance with the words and teaching of Jesus, outlined throughout the sermon, is absolutely crucial. The emphasis is on *these words of mine*. It is the teaching of Jesus, not the Law, which must be taken seriously and must be the foundation of our living.[66] The two outcomes refer to the final, eschatological reckoning. The houses look very much the same; it is at the final judgement that the difference will become evident.

In Luke's Gospel, you will recall that when a woman in the crowd pronounces Mary blessed because she is the mother of Jesus, Jesus highlights that it is her hearing and keeping God's word that matters, and is the source of her blessedness. On another occasion he states that,

> Here are my mother and my brothers! For whoever does the will of my Father in heaven is my brother and sister and mother. (Matt 12:46-50)

This, then, is to build on firm foundations; solid as a rock. The alternative – listening and failing to act – is a recipe for disaster, building on sand which hasn't stability and can't resist the storms which come.[67] The concluding phrase has an ominous ring.

Reflections

Words, theological discourse, instruction, exhortation and retreat talks are great – but, at the end of the day, it is the quality of our living and loving which matters. Towards the end of his Gospel, Matthew includes what is usually called the parable of the last judgment. Jesus makes it clear that the key criterion, the crucial benchmark, is practical love for others, and he provides a list of examples: feeding the hungry, giving drink to the thirsty, clothing the naked, visiting the sick and imprisoned. He refers a little earlier to the weightier commands of the Torah: *justice, mercy and faith.*

The Father's will is summed up in the twin commandment to love.[68] Paul sings from the same hymn sheet when writing to the community in Corinth. It's fine to have the gift of tongues or prophetic powers, to have theological knowledge, even strong faith – but it's worth nothing if we are people who haven't learned to love. He provides a wonderful synthesis of what loving means in practice: patience, kindness, avoiding resentfulness and irritability, not boasting or being arrogant.[69]

Advent is an invitation, an opportunity to listen to God's word and reflect on it, to enrich mind and heart. But it is also an occasion for an honest look at the way we are living and are relating to others. We are urged to examine the foundations of the building we are constructing through our living, and make sure that it is Christ who is at the base. Otherwise we are walking on shifting and dangerous sands, like the treacherous stretches in the Morecambe Bay area. This isn't a good idea. It also misses the whole point of our life and of our discipleship. Let's make sure that it is love which is at the centre of whatever we construct in our lives.

Jesus Cures the Blind

One of the great Advent and Christmas themes is the symbol of light and its opposite, the darkness. In my part of the world the time of year facilitates the symbolism. This is one of the many elements in the first reading from Isaiah: after shadow and darkness, the eyes of the blind will see. It is this aspect of the Isaian extract which is picked up and developed in the Gospel episode.[70]

> As Jesus went on from there, two blind men followed him, crying loudly, *Have mercy on us, Son of David!* When he entered the house, the blind men came to him; and Jesus said to them, *Do you believe that I am able to do this?* They said to him, *Yes, Lord.* Then he touched their eyes and said, *According to your faith let it be done to you.* And their eyes were opened. Then Jesus sternly ordered them, *See that no one knows of this.* But they went away and spread the news about him throughout that district. (Matt 9:27-31)

There are several other Gospel stories which could be chosen to illustrate this theme: the two-stage healing as described in Mark, or the cure of Bartimaeus near Jericho, or of the man born blind as recounted in the Gospel of John.[71] The episode chosen for today's reading is an extract from Matthew's Gospel. It is situated in the third cluster of the miracle stories grouped together by the evangelist to illustrate that Jesus is not only the messianic teacher, but also the messianic healer.[72] As often is the case in Matthew, in his story there are two blind men who follow Jesus as he heads for home, rather than a single individual.[73] As they follow him along the road, they shout loudly for mercy, *Take pity on us*, addressing Jesus as *Son of David*.[74] This title refers to Jesus as the messianic healer.[75]

Blindness in that culture entailed not only poverty, hardship and a degree of isolation, but also religious alienation, for it was often considered to be a punishment for sin.[76] Jesus walks on until he reaches the door of his home base, probably Peter's house. The two catch up with him there. He is obviously aware of what they seek; there is no need for them to ask. The issue highlighted is whether they believe that he is able to do what they want. Jesus asks the challenging question clearly: *Do you believe I can do this?*[77] In response to their affirmative reply, Jesus reaches out compassionately and touches their eyes. His comment underlines the importance of faith: *Your faith deserves it, so let this be done for you.* Their sight is immediately restored. They ignore the strong injunction of Jesus that they should keep the matter quiet, for they spread news of the event throughout the district. It is impossible to stifle the Good News of the Kingdom. The impact of Jesus' mission is widening.[78]

Reflections

Blindness is a terrible affliction, a great burden to have to bear. The gift of sight is one of the most wonderful gifts with which most of us have been endowed. Effortlessly, our eyes catch the beauty of the world around us in its bewildering variety of hue, shape, texture and movement. We can distinguish the shades of green in the trees, the shades of grey in the clouds. We can appreciate the bright and subtle colours of the flowers and birds. We can appreciate the skill of artists as they seek to capture and hold such beauty in oils, pastels and watercolours. We can stand in bewilderment when choosing curtains or wallpaper or paint for our home. We can scan people's faces, sensitive to details of uniqueness and mood, the warmth in a smile, the twinkle in an eye, the sadness on a brow. We can experience the contemplative fascination of the play of light and shade on a hillside or in a lake. Sight brings such richness and meaning to our lives. As we imagine the joy of the men in the story, perhaps we can pause to thank God that we can see, and resolve not to take this wonderful gift for granted.

Light and darkness are not just physical realities; they are symbols of our inner life too, pointers to insight and to ignorance. We have been exposed to light for the mind and heart also, through books, poetry, plays, cinema, TV and music; now through surfing the net. In these we have encountered darkness too. In our lives we have listened to sermons and attended lectures. We have read articles and books, received counsel and advice. We have spent time in prayer. We have engaged in conversation and discussion. Opportunities for enlightenment have been numerous. How rich is our vision, how deep our understanding, how strong our commitment? Perhaps, like the disciples of the Gospels, we stumble along, sometimes in the light, sometimes in the shadows. There are things about Jesus which perhaps are something of a puzzle. There are aspects of discipleship with which we struggle. Though we are not blind, our sight is impaired and partial still. Like the two men in our narrative, we ask Jesus to enable us to see; to see more clearly and more truly. We pray for firmer faith and stronger commitment in following him.

As we seek to follow Jesus as his disciples and friends, we are doubtless aware that there are areas of our being, dimensions of our selfhood, aspects of our living, which the light has not yet penetrated. There is a shadow side of our personality, a darkness which seeks to overcome the light. There may even be pockets of darkness which we prefer to defend and perpetuate. We can make wrong judgements, be narrow and closed in our attitudes. We can take wrong turnings on our journey, walking uncertainly in the shadows. We can still be blind, at least sometimes and in some areas of life. And there is much darkness in our wider world: lies and deception; oppression, violence and injustice; hatred and prejudice. There are elements of darkness in our Church and in our communities, parishes and families. In this time of Advent, we offer God our thanks, and we also acknowledge our need for light and healing and deeper faith. We get in touch with Israel's ancient longing and the longing of the blind of the Gospel. We pray that we will be sources of light for one another, for those whose lives we touch.

Jesus Sends out His Disciples on Mission

The Gospel extract for today continues Matthew's presentation of the story of Jesus. After the series of detailed examples of the healing ministry of Jesus, some of which we have just considered, he provides a brief but telling résumé of the activity of Jesus as he proclaims the Kingdom and makes it present.[79] It shows how Jesus fulfils the vision of Isaiah included in the first reading, which emphasises the graciousness of God who dresses the wounds of his people.[80]

So Jesus went round all the towns and villages teaching in their synagogues, proclaiming the good news of the Kingdom, and curing every kind of illness and infirmity. The sight of the crowds moved him to pity: they were like sheep without a shepherd, harassed and helpless. Then he said to his disciples, *The crop is heavy, but the labourers too few; you must ask the owner to send labourers to bring in the harvest.*

Then Jesus summoned his twelve disciples and gave them authority over unclean spirits, to cast them out, and to cure every disease and every sickness.

These twelve Jesus sent out with the following instructions: *Go nowhere among the Gentiles, and enter no town of the Samaritans, but go rather to the lost sheep of the house of Israel. As you go, proclaim the good news, "The kingdom of heaven has come near." Cure the sick, raise the dead, cleanse the lepers, cast out demons. You received without payment; give without payment.*

(Matt 9:35-10:1,5-8)

Crowds have been in attendance during the Sermon on the Mount. In fact, it was the sight of them, having come from nearby places and from further afield, which stimulated Jesus to address them.[81]

31

They have been present too for many of Jesus' miracles. Sometimes their response has been enthusiastic, sometimes ambivalent.[82] Yet, it is once again the condition of the crowds which moves Jesus to compassion.[83] For they are *harassed and helpless, like sheep without a shepherd*. There is a leadership vacuum; this is an implicit critique of the performance of those in positions of power and responsibility.[84] The situation of the peasants in Galilee is extremely difficult. They are victims, needing someone to guide, support and champion them. More important than their physical needs and concerns is, *The great spiritual need of the people, whose lives have no centre, whose existence seems aimless, whose experience is one of futility.*[85] The imagery of shepherdless sheep is heavy with Old Testament associations.[86] Wandering around the villages, Jesus has become increasingly aware of their pitiful and needy state. He is deeply concerned for their welfare. His heart goes out to them. His compassion is that of a genuine shepherd. Back in the Infancy Narrative at the beginning of the Gospel, Matthew introduced Jesus in the words of the prophets as, *The ruler who will shepherd my people Israel.*[87] It is that role which Jesus is fulfilling through his care for the people.[88]

His response to this situation is twofold. Firstly, switching imagery, he states that, *The harvest is plentiful but the labourers are few.*[89] He urges the disciples to pray that the Lord will send out labourers into the harvest. The people, like a field waiting to be harvested, need to be exposed to the Good News about the Kingdom, and gathered into it, experiencing its presence. Secondly, their prayer is answered instantly.[90] Since, *Prayer to God is not an excuse for inaction, but a challenge to dedicated enterprise for him,*[91] Jesus moves into action, calling the twelve to him.[92] He gives them his authority to cast out evil spirits and cure all kinds of sickness and disease, freely dispensing the blessings of the Kingdom-gift which they have themselves freely experienced.[93]

His compassion urges him to associate others with him in ministering to them. These Jesus sent out. Their ministry is an extension of his; they do what he does. The driving force behind the activity of Jesus and the whole missionary enterprise, in which his disciples share, is his compassion. His compassion aligns him with the *hesed* of Yahweh; it identifies Jesus as the promised Davidic Messiah, the Shepherd leader of Israel.[94]

The instructions which Jesus gives form the introduction to what is commonly referred to as the missionary discourse. Jesus clearly prescribes limitations to their enterprise, boundaries not to be crossed at this stage in the proclamation of the Kingdom. The focus, picking up the Shepherd imagery again, is on the lost sheep of the house of Israel. The Samaritans and the Gentiles are not included; both these groups were despised in first century Judaism. In the course of the ministry, as we have seen in the story of the healing of the centurion's servant, there are exceptions.[95] The restriction is finally lifted when the risen Jesus sends the disciples to all the nations of the world.[96] For the time being, Jesus is most concerned about the dire need of his own people, God's chosen. His concern underlines God's faithfulness to His covenant promises.

The main focus of their mission is like that of Jesus, to proclaim the advent of the Kingdom; the ministry of healing, raising the dead and casting out devils are the symbolic expression of the Kingdom's presence.[97]

Reflections

The key theme of compassion, which we touched on earlier in our Wednesday reflection, returns in today's reading. It is often linked with the symbolism of shepherding, as in the current passage. When considering the idea of Jesus as our shepherd, we naturally tend to think of the beautiful section of the Fourth Gospel in which Jesus claims to be the good or ideal shepherd. But it is a theme which runs through Matthew's Gospel too. For this evangelist Jesus is our shepherd leader who throughout his ministry reaches out in compassionate care to comfort and heal the people.

At the end of the Gospel he gathers his scattered sheep on the mountain and commissions them to proclaim the Gospel to all the nations.

Perhaps in our Advent prayer we could dwell on the fact that Jesus is with us as our shepherd. The beautiful Psalm 23, *The Lord is my Shepherd*, with which we are familiar, suggests phrases to ponder: *he revives my drooping spirit; he leads me in the right path; he is with me; he prepares a table for me; my cup overflows.* Isaiah describes God in these words: *Like a shepherd he will tend his flock and with his arm keep them together; he will carry the lambs in his bosom and lead the ewes to water.*[98] The prophet Micah's words about Bethlehem included in the Magi story I find very helpful: *From you will come a leader who will shepherd my people Israel.* Jesus is my shepherd leader or guide each day. Jesus makes present the shepherding love of God, so movingly described by Ezekiel: *He will himself go to their rescue, and seek out the lost, bind up the crippled, strengthen the weak, watch over the fat and strong, bring the strays back, and provide excellent pasture.*[99]

At the same time Advent invites us to reflect on our own shepherding role as disciples of Jesus. This applies in so many areas of our living: parents and grandparents in the family, teachers and youth leaders in formal and informal educational settings, bishops and priests with their people, doctors, nurses and carers with their patients, managers with their staff. Following the lead of Jesus, we are called to relate with kindness and consideration, be concerned about people's safety, security and freedom, provide nourishment for mind, body and spirit, have particular care for the broken, disabled and vulnerable, and seek to bring healing and wholeness.[100]

Endnotes

1. On Matthew's Gospel I have found the following books helpful: W.F. Albright and C.S. Mann, Matthew (New York, Doubleday 1971); F.W. Beare, *The Gospel according to Matthew* (Oxford, Blackwell 1981); B. Byrne, *Lifting the Burden* (Collegeville, Liturgical Press 2004); Cabrido J.A., *The Shepherd of Israel for All Nations. A Portrayal of Jesus in the Gospel of Matthew: a Narrative-Critical and Theological Study*, (S.T.D. diss., Pontifical Gregorian University, 2008); W.D. Davis and D.C. Allison, *A Critical and Exegetical Commentary on the Gospel according to Saint Matthew* (London, T&T Clark 2004); H.B. Green, *The Gospel according to Matthew* (London, OUP 1975); R.H. Gundry, *Matthew* (Grand Rapids, Eerdmans 1982); D.A. Hagner, *Matthew*, 2 vols (Nashville, Nelson 2000); D.J. Harrington, *The Gospel of Matthew* (Collegeville, Liturgical Press 1991); C.S. Keener, *A Commentary on the Gospel of Matthew* (Grand Rapids, Eerdmans 1999); U. Luz, *The Theology of the Gospel of Matthew* (Cambridge, CUP 1995); M. McKenna, *Matthew the Book of Mercy* (New York, New City Press 2007); J.P. Meier, *Matthew* (Dublin, Veritas 1980); P.S. Minear, *Matthew, The Teacher's Gospel* (London, DLT 1982); F.J. Moloney, *This is the Gospel of the Lord* (Year A) (Homebush, St. Paul 1992); E. Schweizer, *The Good News according to Matthew* (London, SPCK 1976); D. Senior, *Matthew* (Nashville, Abingdon Press 1998); N.T. Wright, *Matthew for Everyone*, 2 vols (London, SPCK 2002).

2. Matt 8:5-13; Luke 7:1-10; this is the only miracle story in the 'Q' tradition which is developed at some length; it seems to be a mixed form: miracle story and pronouncement. See J.P. Meier, *A Marginal Jew*, 3 vols (Doubleday, New York 1994), 2:718; 764, fn178. Hagner, 1:202, sees it as a miracle story transformed by Matthew into a pronouncement story, where the main point is the teaching in vv.10-12. The Fourth Evangelist has a similar story involving a *royal official* and his son; this is situated in Cana, and has literary and structural

ties with the earlier Cana incident, when Jesus changes water into wine at a wedding. See M.T. Winstanley, *Symbols and Spirituality* (Bolton, Don Bosco Publications 2008), p.98. It is probably a variant of an original episode in Jesus' ministry. F.J. Moloney, *John* (Collegeville, Liturgical Press 1998), p.153, 160-161, argues persuasively that this man is a Gentile, though not all agree (see Meier, 2:722).

3. In the structure of Matthew's Gospel there are five discourses of Jesus: the Sermon on the Mount (5:1-7:29), the discourse on mission (9:35-10:42), the parables (13:1-52), the discourse on life in the Church community (18:1-35), the final discourse on the challenge and hope of the future (24:1-25:46). Some scholars maintain that this fivefold structure is modelled on the Pentateuch.

4. This is the only miracle story in Matthew which is not found in Mark.

5. Matthew, in the first verse of his Gospel, introduces Jesus as Messiah, the one who fulfils the expectations of his people, which developed over the centuries. This fulfilment Matthew illustrates in his narrative of the ministry. By the time of Jesus Israel's expectations took a variety of forms; a uniform or dominant one was lacking.

6. S. Voorwinde, *Jesus' Emotions in the Gospels* (London, T&T Clark 2011), p.16.

7. See Meier, *Matthew*, p.79-81; Harrington, p.115; Albright & Mann, p.94; Byrne, p.74.

8. Meier, *Marginal*, 2:721, notes that most centurions were ordinary soldiers who progressed through the ranks; the number of troops they commanded varied; it could be 30 or 60 men. They exercised more than simply military duties, including building and diplomatic roles. They are not a homogeneous group. Herod Antipas had a private army, probably consisting mainly of Gentiles, and adopted Roman military nomenclature. Their role was to control Galilee. Harrington, p.113, raises the possibility that the man could be retired. Hagner, 1:203, maintains that the garrison was probably Roman, and the centurion too. This is contrary to Meier's view. Schweizer, p.213, opts for Syrian origin.

9. *Lord* is polite and respectful; for Christian readers it would have greater significance. Hagner, 1:204, suggests that the centurion regarded Jesus as a person uniquely endowed by God with authority. Matthew's Greek (*pais*) is ambiguous, perhaps reflecting earlier Aramaic ambiguity, and can mean servant or son; the evangelist does not resolve the ambiguity. Most commentators and translations opt for *servant*; Green, p.99, prefers *son*, as do Hagner, 1:204 and Luz, given the centurion's deep concern. The versions of Luke (*doulos*), a servant, and John (*huios*), a son, reflect different interpretations. In Luke and John the problem is that the servant or son is near to death, in Luke with some unspecified illness, in John with a fever; in Matthew he is painfully paralysed, but not in danger of death.

10. Albright & Mann, p.93.

11. Voorwinde, p.19, notes that the centurion has authority because he is under (imperial) authority; Jesus is similarly under divine authority. Jesus is backed by God's authority. Green, p.99, also notes the analogy.

12. Voorwinde, p.18-19; Harrington, p.113, and Green, p.99, take this view; also Davies & Allison, p.120. Senior, p.98, follows most commentators in opting for the traditional opinion; also Schweizer, p.213; Hill, p.158; Hagner, 1:204, as Matthew is similar to Luke in this. Beare, p.207, believes the view is over-subtle; in Matthew Jesus usually takes the initiative and sets his own course. Gundry, p.143, rejects the indignant question idea. Meier, *Marginal*, 2:719 fn182, outlines in detail the issues involved, but concludes by disagreeing with the view. One strong reason is Jesus' immediate response to the marginalised leper in the previous incident, infringing the Law in the process; the two stories are in parallel. Also, the centurion is not bargaining for an alternative, but is humbly waiving the favour spontaneously offered by Jesus. The idea of Jesus going to the house was not part of the centurion's original request, and so cannot be a cause of indignation.

13. Also Mark 6:6; in Mark and here in Matthew, Jesus' amazement is a response to the presence or absence of faith.

Usually the verb (*thaumazein*) applies to other people: the disciples in Matt 8:27; 21:20; the crowds in 9:33; 15:31; the Pharisees in 22:22; Pilate 27:14. Matthew rarely refers to Jesus' emotions.

14. In Luke 13:28-29, the saying in v.11-13 is a separate saying of Jesus in a different context, and is not linked with the miracle story; the reference to Israel precedes mention of the Gentiles, the reverse of Matthew. Meier, *Matthew*, p.84; Senior, p.99; Hagner, 1:205, maintain that Matthew has added these verses (11-13) from 'Q' to the original healing story. The OT expectation was that Gentiles would make pilgrimage to Jerusalem as witnesses rather than participants in the banquet. Those coming from east and west referred to the return of *diaspora* Jews. Matthew's view is radically different. The apocalyptic imagery of *outer darkness, weeping, and gnashing of teeth* are typical Matthaean judgement metaphors. Senior, p.99, notes the view that in their original context these words may have applied to *diaspora* Jews responding to the Gospel more readily than those living in Judea. In Matthew's context the contrast is between Jew and Gentile. See also Davies & Allison, p.121.

15. Isa 25:6-8; 49:12; Mal 1:11. Luz, *Theology*, p.73, states that in the context of Matthew's Gospel these words become a proclamation of disaster foretelling what actually will happen, since the vast majority of Israel did not find faith in Jesus.

16. Luz, *Theology*, p.73, writes that this single episode foretells the future salvation of the Gentiles as a whole. In this respect it has the character of a 'signal'.

17. 12:15-21, quoting Isa 42:1-4; see Byrne, p.77.

18. 24:14

19. 15:24; see also 10:5-6.

20. 28:18-19

21. Meier, *Matthew*, p.84; Schweizer, p.215-216.

22. Beare, p.206; Hagner, 1:206.

23. Davies & Allison, p.121.

24. Beare, p.209.

25. Based on Matt 8:8.

26. On Luke see: B. Byrne, *The Hospitality of God* (Collegeville, Liturgical Press 2000); G.C. Caird, *St. Luke* (London, Pelican 1963); E.E. Ellis, *The Gospel of Luke* (London, Oliphants 1974); C.F. Evans, *Saint Luke* (London, SCM 1990); J.A Fitzmyer, *The Gospel according to Luke* (New York, Doubleday, vol 1 1981, vol 2 1985); J.B. Green, *The Gospel of Luke* (Eerdmans, Grand Rapids 1999); L.T. Johnson, *The Gospel of Luke* (Collegeville, Liturgical Press 1991); M.Fallon, *Gospel according to St Luke* (Bangalore, Asian Trading Corporation 1997); I.H. Marshall, *The Gospel of Luke* (Exeter, Paternoster Press 1978); F. Mosetto, *Lettura del Vangelo secondo Luca* (Rome, LAS 2003), D. McBride, *The Gospel of Luke* (Dublin, Dominican Publications 1991). G.H.P. Thompson, *The Gospel according to Luke* (Oxford, Clarendon 1972); N.T. Wright, *Luke for Everyone* (London, SPCK 2001).

27. *Now it happened that as the time drew near for him to be taken up, he resolutely turned his face towards Jerusalem...*(9:51) Some scholars maintain that the motif continues as far as 19:44.

28. At 9:57, *As they travelled along*; 10:38, *In the course of their journey he came to a village*; 13:22, *Through towns and villages he went*; 17:11, *Now on the way to Jerusalem he travelled along the border between Samaria and Galilee*; 18:31, *Now we are going up to Jerusalem*; 19:11, *He was near Jerusalem*; 19:28, *He went on ahead, going up to Jerusalem*; 19:37, *And now, as he was approaching the downward slope of the Mount of Olives*; 19:41, *As he drew near and came in sight of the city*; 19:45, *Then he went into the Temple.*

29. 1:47; Acts 2:26; 16:34. In today's first reading Isaiah states that on the shoot sprung from the stock of Jesse *the spirit of the Lord rests* (11:1-2).

30. 3:21-22; 5:15; 6:12; 9:18; 9:28-29.

31. 11:2-4. Other references to the prayer of Jesus occur in the Passion Narrative: Jesus prays for Simon Peter at the Supper (22:31-34); the agony prayer on the Mount of Olives (22:39-46); the Calvary prayer of forgiveness (23:34); Jesus' dying prayer (23:46). Luke provides us with a number of sayings and parables of Jesus concerning prayer: the parable of the friend at midnight (11:5-8); sayings about asking and seeking (11:9-13); the parable of the judge and the widow (18:1-8);

the parable of the Pharisee and the tax collector (18:9-14); the exhortation to his disciples to pray and not lose heart (18:1); the exhortation in Jerusalem (21:36); the exhortation on the Mount of Olives (22:40).

32. Many psalms contain the words *I thank you that...* followed by the reason (Psa 78:1; 138:1); this is the pattern also of the *Magnificat* and *Benedictus* earlier in the Gospel. Marshall, p.432, detects in this section a background of Jewish wisdom literature.

33. Marshall, p.433, holds that Jesus uses the *Abba* address to the Father, as do children to their dad.

34. Marshall, p.434, suggests that the concealing is perhaps not to be stressed.

35. The religious elite of Jesus' day, despite their learning, have failed to recognise what is happening in Jesus.

36. 1:51-53; 4:18-19; see also 1Cor 1:18-31.

37. See especially chapter 17, the prayer of Jesus at the Supper.

38. The verb *handed over* can be used of the handing down of knowledge or the transfer of power and authority. Probably both authority and knowledge are meant here.

39. Some scholars (Thompson, p.163 amongst them) think that the relationship between God and Israel (described as father and son) is in the background.

40. In Matthew the next verses are presented in a different context, after the parable of the sower (13:16-17). This is the seventh *macarism* or beatitude of the Gospel.

41. Green, p.423-424.

42. Exod 3:5

43. See, for instance, Isa 25:6; Joel 4:18; Amos 9:13.

44. Exod 19:3

45. Davies & Allison, p.259, stress the Mount Zion typology.

46. Isa 25:6-10; also Isa 35:5-6.

47. For example in Isa 25:22 and Ezek 27:32.

48. M E Boring, *Mark* (Louisville, Westminster John Knox Press 2006), p.209.

49. Cabrido, p.13, and fn8. He makes the point that Jesus has already shown openness to Gentiles (8:5-13; 8:28-9:1).

50. 4:8; 5:1; 14:23; 15:29; 17:1; 21:1; 26:30; 28:16. Jesus sits, as in 5:1, the Sermon on the Mount.

51. Meier, *Matthew*, p.174, notes that this is the last summary of the Galilean ministry (see 4:23-25; 8:16-17; 9:35; 14:14); it is meant to portray the successful climax of Jesus' ministry there. Scholars note the background of Isa 35:5-6: *Then the eyes of the blind will be opened and the ears of the deaf unstopped; then the lame shall leap like the deer, and the tongue of the speechless sing for joy.* Cabrido, p.15, also indicates Isa 26:19; 29:18f; Jesus fulfils Messianic expectations. The summary replaces Mark's story of the healing of a deaf-mute.

52. Senior, p.184-185; Byrne, p.125.

53. Voorwinde, p.34.

54. Isa 29:23. Beare, p.346, comments that this phrase is used in the NT only here and Luke 1:68; he wonders whether there is a hint that those healed are Gentiles, and this carries over into the next feeding episode. Davies & Allison, p.259, note that the phrase is often used in the OT on the lips of Jews (Exod 5:1; 1Kings 1:48; Psa 41:13; Isa 29:23), often in liturgical contexts, and cannot be used as evidence of a Gentile crowd. Similarly Hagner, p.446.

55. Meier, *Matthew*, p.175, sees this story as a doublet of Matt 14:13-21, the feeding of the 5000. Along with Voorwinde, p.34-39; Wright, 1:204; Davies & Allison, p.258, he does not think that Matthew intends this feeding to be for Gentiles, as does Mark. Green, p.148, would disagree. Hagner, p.452, maintains that the story intimates the extension of messianic and eschatological blessing even to the Gentiles.

56. Davies & Allison, p.258-261; Wright picks this up also in 1:204-205. Cabrido, p.15-17, also stresses the eschatological flavour of the passage.

57. The verb is *eucharistein*. There is no reference to the blessing and distribution of the fish, which accentuates the link with the celebration of the eucharist in the community.

58. *Eschatological* refers to the end-time. Davies & Allison, p.261, stress that in this second feeding incident, Matthew is interested in bringing out the idea that in Jesus the Messiah the eschatological promises surrounding Zion have begun

to be fulfilled: the gathering of Jewish crowds (Jer 31:10-13; Ezek 34:14,26-27), the healing of the sick, the allusion to Isa 35:5-6 (also Jer 31:8; Mic 4:6-7), the feeding of many, and the mountain setting (Isa 25:6-10; Jer 31:12-14), are all at home in Jewish texts about Mount Zion. Mount Zion typology is strong here. Perhaps, for Matthew, Jesus has replaced Zion as the centre of God's dealings with God's people. Hagner, p.445, is open to the Zion symbolism. Senior, p.185, notes the links with the wilderness feeding of Israel in the past, and the eucharistic celebration of the community.

59. Cabrido, p.17.

60. 11:1

61. Most commentators make this connection and the link with the eschatological banquet; see, for instance, Davies & Allison, p.258.

62. See McKenna, p.140.

63. Luke's simpler version of the parable at the conclusion of the sermon on the plain describes the first building with greater detail; the second building has no foundation at all; the problem is simply a swollen river (6:48-49). The two evangelists perhaps reflect different topographical and climatic conditions and experience.

64. Matthew concludes the other discourses of the Gospel with similar warnings for those who fail to put Jesus' teaching into practice; see Senior, p.89.

65. The word for *wise* or *prudent* (*phronimos*) is a favourite term for Matthew; the same contrast between wise and foolish is found in the parable of the young women (25:1-13).

66. See also John 13:17; James 1:22-25.

67. Green, p.97, notes that in Palestine floods were not uncommon after the autumn rains. Hagner, p.191, observes how the blasting winds and torrential rains transform the dry wadis and produce flash floods. The storm imagery is frequent in the OT (Isa 28:2; Ezek 13:10).

68. 23:23; 22:37-40.

69. 1 Cor 13:4-7.

70. Isa 29:18; 35:5;42:.7

71. Mark 8:22-26; 10:46-52; John 9:1-41.
72. See earlier in the chapter. The story is also a preparation for 11:5, the Baptist's question.
73. Beare, p.236, considers the story a doublet of the later healing outside Jericho; there too there are two men involved; Green, p.105, believes it is a variant. Hagner, p.252, suggests that some common elements may result from a crossover in language between the passages. The detail about the house suggests an independent story.
74. In the OT this title was used only of Solomon, who was renowned as a healer and exorcist. In the Jericho passage the same form of address is used. Hagner, p.232, disagrees with the Solomon connection (*pace* Davies & Allison, p.142).
75. Meier, *Matthew*, p.99. Senior, p.109, sees it as a messianic title (see 12:23; 15:22; 20:30,31). His messianic power is an expression of his compassion and humility.
76. Davies & Allison, p.142; Hagner, p.253, refers to social outcasts.
77. Hagner, p.254, maintains that this is the only place in the Gospel tradition that Jesus asks someone whether they believe that he has power to heal them.
78. Senior, p.109.
79. The introductory verse is a *verbatim* replica of an earlier summary (4:23). Scholars refer to this as an inclusion. Meier, *Matthew,* p.100-101, refers to 'Janus-like buffer sections'.
80. Isa 30:19-21, 23-26.
81. Senior, p.112. See also 8:1; 9:33.
82. Voorwinde, p.26.
83. The Greek verb means moved to the depths of one's being; it is applied to Jesus by Matthew also in 14:14; 15:32; 20:34, and occurs in a parable in 18:27.
84. Senior, p.113; Davies & Allison, p.146.
85. Hagner, p.260.
86. Num 27:17 (Moses & Joshua); 1 Kings 22:17 (Ahab); also 2 Chr 18:16; Zech 13:7 applied to Jesus' disciples in 26:31; Isa 53:6; Ezek 34.
87. 2:6

88. In 8:17 Matthew quotes Isa 53:4: *he took our infirmities and bore our diseases.*

89. Usually this harvest imagery evokes judgement (Isa 18:4; 24:13; 27:12; Jer 51:53; Hos 6:11; Joel 3:13); here it is a metaphor for mission; see Davies & Allison, p.146. The eschatological harvest has been moved to the present. Hill, p.182, sees their role as warning men of the approach of the judgement and calling them to repentance. But Hagner, p.260, maintains that it cannot here mean eschatological judgement, though the urgency remains. For Meier, *Matthew,* p.101, the mission of the disciples is part of the eschatological event.

90. Wright, 1:110, notes that often we are ourselves part of God's answer to our prayers!

91. Beare, p.238.

92. Our current reading omits verses 2-4 in which the names of the apostles (the only time this term is used in Matthew) are listed. Recalling the 12 tribes, they are to be the nucleus of the renewed and restored Israel.

93. The same terminology is found of Jesus in 4:23; 9:35. Jesus does not mention teaching until 28:20. Byrne, p.86, sees the choice and mission of the twelve as the first stage in the reconstitution of Israel.

94. Cabrido, p.7; see Ezek 34:23.

95. 2:1-12; 3:9; 8:10-11; 15:21-28

96. 28:19-20. Senior, p.115, sees these as 'hints of the still unfolding future'. Meier, *Matthew,* p.107, suggests that the prohibition may stem from the historical Jesus; but the words may also have been used by conservative Jewish Christians rejecting the Gentile mission (also Schweizer, p.235).

97. 3:3; 4:17. See Hagner, p.271.

98. Isa 40:11

99. Ezek 34:11-16

100. See Winstanley, *Symbols and Spirituality,* p.89-93; David O'Malley, *Christian Leadership* (Bolton, Don Bosco Publications 2007), p.82-93.

Week Two

Monday - Week Two

The Healing of the Paralysed Man

The first reading today from Isaiah is so beautiful, as the prophet articulates the dreams and longings of his people in vivid imagery: wilderness wastelands, dried-up places are now blooming with bright flowers; deserts are filled with rushing water; weary limbs are strengthened, faint hearts encouraged; the blind and the deaf are healed; there is no longer the threat of wild beasts; and instead of laments and sorrow there is joy and gladness and rejoicing. All these are different images which are intended to communicate a sense of the transformation which God will eventually bring about when the time of redemption and new life comes.

The Gospel reading shows that this time has, in fact, come in the presence and ministry of Jesus.

One day, while he was teaching, Pharisees and teachers of the law were sitting nearby (they had come from every village of Galilee and Judea and from Jerusalem); and the power of the Lord was with him to heal. Just then some men came, carrying a paralysed man on a bed. They were trying to bring him in and lay him before Jesus; but finding no way to bring him in because of the crowd, they went up on the roof and let him down with his bed through the tiles into the middle of the crowd in front of Jesus. When he saw their faith, he said, *Friend, your sins are forgiven you.* Then the scribes and the Pharisees began to question, *Who is this who is speaking blasphemies? Who can forgive sins but God alone?* When Jesus perceived their questionings, he answered them, *Why do you raise such questions in your hearts? Which is easier, to say, "Your sins are forgiven you", or to say, "Stand up and walk?"*

46

But so that you may know that the Son of Man has authority on earth to forgive sins – he said to the one who was paralysed – *I say to you, stand up and take your bed and go to your home.* Immediately he stood up before them, took what he had been lying on, and went to his home, glorifying God. Amazement seized all of them, and they glorified God and were filled with awe, saying, *We have seen strange things today.*

(Luke 5:17-26)

It's a well-known story, this particular manifestation of the wider healing ministry of Jesus. Luke is probably basing himself on the more detailed version of Mark.[1] In the immediate context, as he sets the scene, he includes for the first time the presence of the Pharisees and teachers of the Law, an official delegation coming from the religious centre of Jerusalem.[2] The indication of their presence as Jesus conducts his ministry of teaching makes their later critical intervention less abrupt than it is in Mark. Luke mentions that the power of the Lord was with Jesus in his healing ministry, recalling the baptism and Nazareth scenes.[3] Through the quoting of Isaiah in the Nazareth synagogue, Jesus clarified his mission as entailing the release of those held captive, and the freeing of the oppressed. This takes place in the current story, where healing and forgiveness are closely interwoven, illustrating dramatically that Jesus has both power to heal and authority to forgive. His liberating response to human need becomes the occasion for conflict.

Our attention is focused firstly on a group of men who approach the place carrying a paralysed individual on a bed. The first obstacle which they encounter in their quest to bring the man to Jesus is the thronging crowd, which blocks their access. But they are determined, and with practical imagination they climb the stairs onto the roof, remove the tiles and lower their friend into Jesus' presence.[4] Their kindness and firm commitment are impressive; nothing seems too much trouble. This is friendship at its best. They also manifest a deep faith in Jesus, in his ability and willingness to help their friend and bring him healing.

They take the risk of appearing quite foolish if Jesus fails to respond positively to their quest.

Jesus immediately recognises their faith, and presumably that of the paralysed man himself.[5] The man's physical condition and his need for healing are obvious. Jesus would be aware of accompanying disabilities: the man cannot live a normal family life; he cannot work and earn a living; nor can he take part in the political, social and religious life of the community to which he belongs. In Israel a person with disabilities was seriously marginalised, and was in fact an outcast. In that culture, physical misfortune was often popularly considered to be the result of sin or a punishment for it; this was a further burden for an individual to carry. But Jesus is aware of a more fundamental need, a greater disability. When approached for a cure, it is to this more fundamental and urgent need that, with intuitive empathy, he turns his attention first.

With authority and warm affection, he speaks the word of forgiveness: *My son, your sins are forgiven,* the prophetic announcement of the inbreak of the Kingdom, God's reign in love, into the contorted frame of the paralytic's life, assuring him of the gift of God's unconditional, saving acceptance. The passive verb, *are forgiven*, indicates that it is by God's action that the man's sins are removed; Jesus on God's behalf can proclaim such forgiveness.[6]

The religious leaders who are present on the sidelines take umbrage at this apparent subverting of the prerogative of God. In their view this amounts to blasphemy. Jesus is aware of their thinking and their antagonism.[7] He rounds on them and poses a counterquestion, whether it is easier to pronounce a word of forgiveness or of healing. As incontrovertible evidence that he has authority to forgive sins, he turns to the man and tells him to pick up his bed and go off home. Immediately, he does so. He is healed, released from his paralysis. He can stand erect, bend and carry; he can hike, and work in the fields, and saw wood; he can stand to his waist in the water and cast a net. His feelings of guilt, inadequacy, frustration, anger, failure, resentment, feelings which must have weighed heavily or torn him apart, are dissipated like the early morning mist on the lake. He is restored to his family and the life of the local community. A new day has dawned. He knows at first hand the full reality of the Kingdom.

The cure confirms the truth and effectiveness of Jesus' word of forgiveness. The liberation from the dominion of evil, the salvation which Jesus brings embraces the whole man: physical, psychological and spiritual.

It is clear that Jesus has authority both to heal and to forgive; the two belong together. As he walks home, the man praises God. The onlookers, aware that something unusual is taking place, are filled with awe and wonder at the unexpected things which have occurred, and they too praise God, thus recognising that God is at work in Jesus. The religious leaders, deeply upset, are left confused and challenged by Jesus' claim and activity.

Reflections

Advent is a time when we are invited to be aware of our poverty and need, and to long for the coming of the Saviour to bring us healing, forgiveness, liberation and new life. There is much in today's Gospel story which can stimulate and help us in this. It isn't too difficult for us to identify with the paralysed man himself. Whilst perhaps not being too impaired physically, we are certainly not entirely whole within ourselves. Our growth can be stunted. We can be held back in our relationships with others, held bound by fear, a sense of inadequacy, or selfishness. Reaching out and involvement can be a challenge. We can be carrying around inner hurts, which fester and occasionally erupt. We need to be set free and made whole and become more fully alive. We may be aware of aspects of our sinfulness which cramp our aliveness, deaden our enthusiasm and hold us bound. In our Advent waiting we know our ongoing need for forgiveness, transformation, and a new beginning.

The friends of the paralysed man raise the issue of the quality of our friendships. Like them, we are called to be open and aware of the needs of others, in our family or local community, or further afield.

The man's friends challenge the level of our generosity and commitment, our creativity in responding. Our task, in compassion and care, is to find ways of bringing the needy to Jesus, to enable them to encounter his healing, forgiving, life-giving love. Advent is an invitation to action as well as to waiting.

Advent is also a time of faith. We are called to trust in God's love, to believe in the willingness and ability of Jesus to bring us healing, to walk alongside us each day, to brighten and transform our lives. Advent is a time for us to acknowledge that we don't have all the answers, that we can't go it alone, that we really do need to reach out to Jesus, and do so with confidence.

The Little Ones

Again we have today a wonderful Isaian reading. We hear God's word of consolation, of comfort and assured forgiveness for His people. We meet the familiar Advent imagery of preparing in the wilderness a way for the Lord, filling in valleys, flattening mountains, building a straight highway. The construction of motorways in recent years makes all this real for us centuries later. There is the contrast between fast-withering flowers and God's lasting word. The joyful messenger loudly proclaims to Jerusalem, from the mountain tops, the coming of the Lord. We find a fascinating contrast between the strident words of power, subjection, victory, trophies, and the gentle, homely language of shepherds and lambs.

It is this shepherd imagery that is taken up in the Gospel reading, in that familiar parable of the one sheep that strays and the shepherd who leaves the others and goes off in search of it, and when he finds it, is filled with great joy. This parable is found in both Luke and Matthew in different contexts and with a different emphasis. The version chosen for today comes from Matthew:

> What do you think? If a shepherd has a hundred sheep, and one of them has gone astray, does he not leave the ninety-nine on the mountains and go in search of the one that went astray? And if he finds it, truly I tell you, he rejoices over it more than over the ninety-nine that never went astray. So it is not the will of your Father in heaven that one of these little ones should be lost.
>
> (Matt 18:11-14)

It is sometimes stated that the parables of Jesus were handed down in the oral tradition without reference to the original context in which they were first spoken, which was no longer known.

In writing their Gospels, it was the evangelists who chose a particular location in their overall literary structure for Jesus' stories. In doing so, they also provided an interpretation of the parable's meaning and an application to the situation of their readership.[8] This parable of the shepherd is a good illustration. In Luke it is part of a trilogy used by Jesus as his response to Pharisee criticism of his offering the hospitality of his table to tax gatherers and sinners. Luke closely links the parable of the shepherd searching for his lost sheep with that of the woman searching for her lost coin. There follows the parable of the father searching for his two lost sons (usually referred to as the parable of the prodigal son). In each case there is the note of celebration. At the end of the first two parables, Luke adds a comment about God's joy at the repentance of sinners. The context for Matthew's version of the parable, on the other hand, is a block of Jesus' teaching addressed to disciples (in a broad sense), dealing with relationships and aspects of life in the community.[9]

This discourse, the fourth in Matthew's Gospel, has to do with aspects of life in the Church community. It can be divided into two parts: the need for humility and concern for the little ones, and ways of handling deviant behaviour in the community.[10] Both sections conclude with a parable. In the first section, which ends with the shepherd parable, Jesus stresses the importance of humility. In response to the disciples' question about who is the greatest in the Kingdom,[11] which reflects their misguided preoccupation with power and position, he places a child in their midst in a symbolic gesture, and asserts emphatically that, *Unless you change and become like little children, you will never enter the Kingdom of Heaven.* A fundamentally different attitude and mindset are required. Jesus then provides the paradoxical answer to the original question: *Whoever becomes humble like this child is the greatest in the kingdom of heaven.* A child in that society had no social standing, so Jesus' response is surprising. The point at issue is not a child's innocence or simplicity, but its humble status and lack of pretension.

The child is *a nobody*.[12] Jesus is subversively challenging the obsessive human tendency to accord great value to rank, status, honour and power (greatness). But the Kingdom of Heaven is not about rank, position, and importance; quite the contrary. The disciples are on the wrong track, and Jesus is turning their expectations upside down.[13] Jesus then adds: *Whoever welcomes one such child in my name welcomes me.* In this transitional verse there is a switch from the seeing the child as model to emphasising the way a child is to be treated. In this he is advocating an attitude of care, concern and respect for children and for the lowly and undistinguished members of the community because he is present in them. This idea is illustrated later in the parable of the great judgement, when the judge responds: *Just as you did it to one of the least of these who are members of my family, you did it to me.*[14]

Jesus next speaks very strongly about placing stumbling blocks in the way of the little ones who believe in him. There is a subtle switch from focusing on *a child* understood literally, to *little ones*; these are probably members of the community of immature faith, or insignificant social status, or the lack of impressive personal gifts.[15] Matthew is probably more concerned with the danger of the fragile Christians being led into error, falling away from God, losing their faith, rather than their being led into bad moral conduct.[16] The value of such people in Jesus' eyes is illustrated by his use of the proverbial expression of a millstone, a large stone worked by a donkey, being fastened around the neck of such perpetrators, and their being thrown into the depths of the sea. Philosophically, Jesus acknowledges that scandals will occur, but the consequences for those responsible will be dire.

The importance of each individual disciple in God's eyes is further emphasised when Jesus stipulates that no disciple should look down on another, or treat another with contempt:

> *Take care that you do not despise one of these little ones; for, I tell you, in heaven their angels continually see the face of my Father in heaven.*

(Matt 18:10)

Each disciple has an advocate in God's presence, a fact which illustrates their great value in the Father's eyes, and demands corresponding care and esteem within the community.

The parable comes next in the sequence and is introduced by a direct question: *What do you think?* The listener is immediately drawn in and engaged. This is followed by a rhetorical question, which expects a positive response; of course a genuine shepherd would do this. Some commentators wonder whether such an action would be normal, and so it is a sign of the immense value of a single stray. Others believe that Jesus' question presupposes that the hearer would not find the action of the shepherd untypical.[17] Matthew's version of the parable omits reference to the shepherd carrying the rescued sheep on his shoulders, or inviting his friends to a celebratory party, details which are found in Luke. Also, the sheep has wilfully strayed and there is no presumption that the search will be successful.[18] Perhaps Matthew identifies the shepherd with Jesus who devotes time and energy in searching for the lost little ones.[19] The shepherd reflects the attitude and action of God, his concern for the little ones.[20] The joy which accompanies the finding and restoration of the sheep is an indication of the sheep's great value in the shepherd's estimation.

The final line contains the application of the parable. Since it is God's will that the little ones should not be lost or perish, disciples, especially the leaders and pastors of the community,[21] must do all in their power to prevent members of the community from straying, and to bring about their restoration when they have strayed, so that they will not perish.

Reflections

Advent is a time for getting in touch with our inner poverty and need as we wait again for the coming of our Saviour. Today's Gospel reading reminds us that such poverty is at the heart of our discipleship. In a world which is caught up in success, possessions, comfort, status and power, we are called to be humble.

Humility isn't exactly a buzz word in the society in which we live. It is the antithesis of the generally held approach to relationships and to life. It is a simple, uncomplicated awareness that who we are and what we have are a gift. It is a recognition of our dependence on God and God's sustaining love. It enables us to place our trust in God's ongoing loving and caring presence in our lives. It spells the rejection of the pursuit of status and rank. It expresses a generous acceptance of who we are.

Genuine humility enables us to treat others with respect. In his teaching, Jesus stresses that such care and respect should be given to the weak and vulnerable in our community and world, *the little ones* as he calls them. This Advent we might examine whether we tend to close our eyes to those whom our society ignores or exploits. There are so many children who are undernourished, or who receive little love. There are the sick and infirm, the elderly, refugees, those out of work or on the streets, those struggling financially, the bereaved and lonely. As followers of Jesus we are called to reach out to these little ones with care and compassion, for they are very dear to our God. We need to make sure that we don't take advantage of people who are in any way weaker than ourselves.

Jesus also exhorts us to seek out those in our community who may have strayed. People drift away from the Church for all kinds of reasons. Sometimes stumbling blocks have been placed in their way by fellow Christians, by people with pastoral responsibility, by harshness and lack of flexibility and understanding by clergy. Many have been deeply hurt. They need to find the compassionate face of God in us. Pope Francis has frequently urged us to reach out to them like the shepherd in the parable.

Rest from Burdens

In today's extract from the prophet Isaiah, God is referred to as the One who gives strength to the wearied and the powerless. This is an appropriate introduction to the very brief Gospel reading. It follows a passage in which Jesus has first praised John the Baptist and then moved on to criticise the lakeside cities for their failure to heed his own preaching and miracles. Jesus next prays in thanksgiving to the Father for having hidden the truth of his message from the intelligent and wise and revealed them to infants. We discussed Luke's version of this passage on the Tuesday of last week. Having highlighted the depth of his relationship with the Father, and his position as unique revealer, Jesus continues in words found only in Matthew:

> *Come to me, all you that are weary and are carrying heavy burdens, and I will give you rest. Take my yoke upon you, and learn from me; for I am gentle and humble in heart, and you will find rest for your souls. For my yoke is easy, and my burden is light.*
>
> (Matt 11: 28-30)

Nowhere is the invitation to follow Jesus more personal and tender than here.[22] In parallel phrases an invitation to discipleship and a promise of rest are twice offered. The concluding sentence too is typical of Hebrew poetry, where the same idea is repeated in different words or images: *yoke/burden, easy/light*. The usual invitation to discipleship in the Gospel narratives is to follow Jesus, to come after him. Here it is *to come to Jesus*. The invitation is broad and general, addressed to those not yet involved, those outside the inner circle.

The opening words reflect Jesus' awareness of the difficult life which so many of the people around him endured. The taxation system imposed by Rome and by Herod was heavy. In some areas many peasants had been dispossessed and work was hard to find.

There was a lot of hunger, real poverty, insecurity and fear. Physically and emotionally, life was burdensome. Throughout the Gospel Jesus is presented as reaching out with compassion and care towards those in need.

In addition, the religious system was quite oppressive. The familiar and vivid image of the kind of wooden yoke, used with oxen in farming, was adapted in the Hebrew Bible as a metaphor to denote teaching or instruction, Wisdom and Law. The rabbis spoke of the Law as the yoke of the Kingdom of God, which men must put on.[23] The emphasis in Jesus' words, then, has a polemical thrust,[24] and has to do mainly with the burden of keeping the Law especially as developed through the complex casuistry and rigorous interpretation of the Pharisees. This had become too detailed and extensive for ordinary folk, the *people of the land*, to cope with. They were despised and marginalised by the religious elite.[25] On another occasion, Jesus accuses the scribes and Pharisees of tying up heavy burdens hard to bear, and laying them on the shoulders of others, without lifting a finger to help.[26]

Jesus is inviting his listeners to accept his teaching, an alternative which is not onerous but is, in fact, liberating. It is his teaching which is now the definitive interpretation of the Law.[27] The Kingdom he so often talks about spells acceptance, forgiveness, and friendship. The God in whose name he speaks is a God of generous love. Jesus himself, unlike the religious leaders of his day, is humble and gentle, unassuming and considerate, in his approach to people.[28] He is described like this later in the narrative.[29] He is an attractive personality, who *embodies all he teaches and commands.*[30]

Jesus promises those who accept his invitation that they will find inner peace (profound *shalom*), fulfilment and salvation; this will be a present prelude to later eschatological blessing. In Exodus God tells Moses, *I will give you rest.*[31] Here, it is Jesus, who is clearly greater than Moses, who takes over that role. The phrasing recalls the prophet Jeremiah: *Stand at the crossroads and look, and ask for the ancient paths where the good way lies; and walk in it, and find rest for your souls.*[32]

There are links with the resting of God after the creation, and the traditional weekly Sabbath resting. It was envisaged that the messianic age would be a time of rest, like a great Sabbath. This expectation is now being fulfilled in and through Jesus.

As part of the rich scriptural background for this Matthaean passage, many scholars detect in Jesus' words echoes of the Book of Sirach:[33]

> Draw near to me, you who are uneducated, and lodge in the house of instruction. Why do you say you are lacking in these things, and why do you endure such great thirst? I opened my mouth and said, *Acquire wisdom for yourselves without money. Put your neck under her yoke, and let your souls receive instruction; it is to be found close by.*
>
> (Sirach 51:23-26)

This suggests that Matthew is here presenting and identifying Jesus as Wisdom. *Jesus stands not only in the place of Wisdom and truth but even in the place of Yahweh.*[34] In this passage Jesus clearly places himself at the centre. There is a strong sense of his personal presence.[35] The link with his previous words concerning his close relationship with the Father is strong. Jesus is the full revelation of God and of the will of God.[36]

Jesus claims that his way is light and easy. Scholars note the inconsistency between the words of Jesus here and the strong demands found in the Sermon on the Mount.[37] His way is certainly demanding, but the context is different, for it is based on a personal relationship of love with Jesus. *When the heart is engaged, when values are lived out within a sense of community that shares and seeks to promote them, then too perhaps an 'ease' and a 'lightness' become palpable.*[38]

Reflections

We all feel burdened at times. Life throws up many challenges, some ongoing and very painful. We find ourselves struggling, weary of it all, longing for a break and some respite and peace. Sometimes the Church can be a support and comfort. Sometimes the Church can actually increase the burdensomeness of our lives. Whilst we do not wish to dilute the vision of Jesus or the values and ideals of his Gospel, there is room for greater realism, compassion and understanding in the practical ways the Church may seek to promote and uphold them.[39]

Much of the burden of life can be the result of the consumer-driven society in which we live: the need to possess more and better, the need to succeed, the need for pleasure and ease. The harsh individualism, the rat race mentality, the lack of compassion and respect in so many areas of our experience increase the burden, bringing additional anxiety and grief. Jesus offers us a different vision and value system, one which emphasises humility, kindness, service. This too makes demands on our time and energy. But we know that a compassionate and servant lifestyle is a sharing in his own way of living and relating, and is a reflection of the being of God.

Jesus invites us this Advent to approach him, to make him the centre of our lives, to commit ourselves again to his way, to surrender to his love and friendship. He promises us an inner peace and calm and serenity that can transform our lives and be a great support for others.

The One who is to Come

One of the great figures in our Advent liturgy is John the Baptiser. He features in several of the Sunday readings, proclaiming the proximity of God's definitive intervention for salvation and judgement.[40] A prophetic figure, puzzling and yet magnetic, he is presented in the Gospels as the one who prepares the way for Jesus. The reading chosen for today's liturgical celebration provides us with Jesus' assessment of him. However, I believe that to understand the text better, it is necessary to examine a more extensive extract of which our text, the third paragraph below, forms an integral part.

When John heard in prison what the Messiah was doing, he sent word by his disciples and said to him, *Are you the one who is to come, or are we to wait for another? Jesus* answered them, *Go and tell John what you hear and see: the blind receive their sight, the lame walk, the lepers are cleansed, the deaf hear, the dead are raised, and the poor have good news brought to them. And blessed is anyone who takes no offence at me.*

As they went away, Jesus began to speak to the crowds about John: *What did you go out into the wilderness to look at? A reed shaken by the wind? What then did you go out to see? Someone dressed in soft robes? Look, those who wear soft robes are in royal palaces. What then did you go out to see? A prophet? Yes, I tell you, and more than a prophet. This is the one about whom it is written, "See, I am sending my messenger ahead of you who will prepare your way before you".*

Truly I tell you, among those born of women no one has arisen greater than John the Baptist; yet the least in the kingdom of heaven is greater than he. From the days of John the Baptist until now the kingdom of heaven has suffered violence, and the violent take it by force. For all the prophets and the law prophesied until John came; and if you are willing to accept it, he is Elijah who is to come. Let anyone with ears listen! (Matt 11: 2-15)

The context in Matthew is the aftermath of the missionary discourse which accompanies the sending out of the disciples to preach and heal in the local villages.[41] There is no explicit mention of the disciples' return. By this time, in the temporal sequence, John has been arrested by Herod and is in prison in Herod's fortified palace on the East shore of the Dead Sea.[42] Presumably, whilst he was in captivity he was allowed visits from his disciples, and has heard from them about the deeds of the Christ, what Jesus is saying and doing.[43] Earlier, on the occasion of Jesus' baptism in the Jordan, John had spoken about a coming one more powerful than he.[44] But he envisaged this figure as involved in God's devastating judgement, and employed the vivid imagery of axes lying ready at the roots of the trees, fruitless trees being burned, threshing floors being cleared and the chaff thrown into the fire, people seeking to flee from the wrath to come. It was apparent that this wasn't happening in the ministry of Jesus. God's enemies were still at large, not least Herod himself. Instead, Jesus is conducting an itinerant preaching mission, and reaching out in kindness and compassion towards the marginalised and sinners.

So John decides to seek clarification, and sends his disciples to him with a question: *Are you the one who is to come, or are we to wait for another?* His question reflects the uncertainty and confusion genuinely afflicting him, uncertainty occasioned by Jesus' different message, style and emphasis in his ministry. Jesus does not quite fit the expectations of his former mentor; he is following a different script. The answer to the question would also have implications for the disciples who conveyed it.[45] Jesus responds:

> Go and tell John what you hear and see: the blind receive their sight, the lame walk, the lepers are cleansed, the deaf hear, the dead are raised, and the poor have good news brought to them. And blessed is anyone who takes no offence at me.

In words with strong echoes of Isaiah,[46] where the prophet describes the kind of blessings which would characterise the messianic age, Jesus points to the evidence at hand in word and deed, the remarkable healings and the freedom and new life they bring, episodes which Matthew has already narrated.[47] What was prophesied is happening. Since Jesus thus fulfils these hopes and dreams, he is clearly the expected one, the Messiah. But Jesus is aware that, despite all that is taking place, there are those who feel confused and find him an obstacle to belief (who are scandalised).[48] But his words here contain a particular appeal and plea to the Baptist and his disciples, who, like many of the people, are expecting a different kind of messianic figure.[49] He should not look for another, *because in that case he is looking for the fulfilment of his own dreams rather than of God's prophecies.*[50] In the storyline there is no reply, only silence.

The focus now switches to the Baptist. If Jesus is in fact the coming one, John's role relative to Jesus requires clarification. Jesus articulates to the crowds how he regards this fascinating figure. He engages them with three rhetorical questions. When they went out enthusiastically in large numbers to the banks of the Jordan to encounter the Baptist, they weren't expecting someone resembling the wild marsh reeds growing there, which waved and bent in the wind.[51] For John consistently and courageously proclaimed a tough and uncompromising message, unlike Herod the fox, whose policies tended to be *flexible*. Nor were they looking for someone dressed in soft robes, an indication of wealth and luxury, as indeed at Herod's court. For John wore a cloak of camel hair and a leather belt and lived rough.[52] On going out to the banks of Jordan the people probably did expect to find a prophetic figure, for he soon came to be understood in those terms. He was indeed a genuine prophet, says Jesus, and, bringing the dialogue to a climax, he adds that John was much more than a prophet.

Quoting the Old Testament, he defines the Baptist as the one sent by God to be the messenger who would prepare the way for Jesus.[53] He is, therefore, the prophet par excellence. He is a pivotal figure, the culmination of the old order, and the forerunner of the new.

It is at this point that the few verses chosen for today's reading commence. Jesus opens quite solemnly: *Truly I say to you*, as he emphatically states that no one greater than John has yet been born. No one in the old order of things is more significant than he. Yet, paradoxically, great as he is, the least person in the Kingdom of Heaven is greater. *His greatness becomes a foil for the surpassing greatness of the kingdom.*[54] The Baptist belongs to the early phase of salvation history, the period of preparation, and that period is now finished. The new era, the time of fulfilment, which is beginning in and through Jesus, and is already present, is vastly superior to the old, and John is not a part of it. Greatness in the Kingdom is not, however, a personal achievement; it is a gift of God freely bestowed.[55]

The following enigmatic verse, in which violence is mentioned, has long been a puzzle to scholars, and its original meaning is probably *irretrievably lost.*[56] From the appearance of the Baptist and on through the ministry of Jesus, there has been opposition to the advent of God's reign.[57] There has been conflict with the demonic world, with the religious leadership, and with Herod. That pattern of opposition and persecution is set to continue.[58] Whereas in the earlier statement the Baptist seems to be excluded from the era of the Kingdom, here he seems to be part of it. An alternative interpretation of the verse suggests that rather than the Kingdom of Heaven suffers violence, the verb should be translated *advances forcefully*, meaning that courageous self-denial and discipline are required of those seeking to become part of it; entry comes at a price. The violent take it by force in the sense that they are prepared to do violence to such things as family feeling in order to enter it.[59]

One of the expectations about the messianic times was that Elijah would come to prepare the end time.[60] Jesus categorically assigns this crucial role to the Baptist, the last in the line of prophetic figures,[61] and the final herald of the Kingdom. In doing so, Jesus is also making clear claims about his own identity and role. This is underlined by his concluding remark, which draws the section to a close, that those with ears to hear should listen attentively.

His listeners should read the implications, should discern the significance of what is happening, and recognise who he is. Later Jesus is even more specific in his identification of Elijah and John, stating that Elijah has already come and they did not recognise him and did to him whatever they pleased.[62]

The block of material which considers the role of the Baptist continues and concludes with the reading chosen for tomorrow.

Reflections

Whilst at first sight it may seem that Matthew is interested in giving information about the Baptist, in fact the focus of his interest is really fixed on Jesus. He highlights Jesus' words and deeds, his key role in the unfolding of salvation history. He makes it quite clear, perhaps bearing in mind the ongoing presence and activity of John's disciples, that the Baptist, great as he is, is subordinate to Jesus as the one who is involved in the final preparation.

In Advent, like the Baptist, we are waiting for the one who is coming. But we are privileged to know his identity, to be conversant with his message, to be acquainted with his style and his characteristic emphases. Yet, it is not impossible that we harbour unrealistic expectations, erroneous preconceptions, or have not put aside hopes and agendas which conflict with his. It is not easy to embrace fully the values of the Kingdom in our thinking and daily living, especially in the context of our modern world. Perhaps there is a sense in which we do take offence at Jesus' message about God's immense love and forgiveness, and at the demands on our generosity and compassion which our God makes.

Whilst there is something wonderful and exciting about our annual preparing for the coming one to arrive again at Christmas, the hoping and waiting can also be uncomfortable. If we allow ourselves to really listen to him, we may be obliged to do some rethinking, to do violence to ourselves, and make some changes to our lifestyle.

The Gospels don't tell us how the Baptist reacted to the message brought back to him by his disciples. Perhaps it was enough to enable him to reshape his expectations and to die in peace, like Simeon in Luke, because he could see that his own and the nation's longings were in fact being fulfilled, albeit in a different way from that which he had envisaged. Perhaps he was able to put his faith in Jesus, and not be scandalised. On the other hand, we have to be open to the possibility that John went to his death still questioning, still unsure about Jesus.[63]

Perhaps Advent invites us to acknowledge the struggles we may have with scandal. This may not be with Jesus but with the Church. We have witnessed the gradual erosion of the hopes and dreams born of Vatican II. Over recent years we have all had to come to terms with the devastating sex abuse scenario. *Vatileaks* has made us more aware of dysfunction and corruption in the Curia. Careerism, power brokering, and control have deprived us of our rights; the message of Jesus concerning self-giving and service seems to have been sidelined or even abandoned. The Church's stand on issues of sexuality, the role of women, divorce and remarriage create stumbling blocks for many. Whilst we firmly believe that we are members of the Kingdom and so are immensely blessed, we know that the Kingdom has not yet fully arrived. And so we wait for the coming of Jesus this Christmastide with great hope and longing. We pray for stronger faith and more generous love.

Dance and Dirge

Isaiah, in today's first reading, explains to the people, on God's behalf, that all would have been well had they been alert to His commands and followed in the way mapped out for them. The accompanying Gospel text for today's liturgy picks up this theme. It is a continuation of yesterday's reading, bringing the discussion of the identity and role of the Baptist to a conclusion. The spotlight is now focused on the response of contemporary Israel to both John and Jesus. Jesus continues speaking:

> But to what will I compare this generation? It is like children sitting in the market-places and calling to one another, *We played the flute for you, and you did not dance; we wailed, and you did not mourn.* For John came neither eating nor drinking, and they say, *He has a demon;* the Son of Man came eating and drinking, and they say, *Look, a glutton and a drunkard, a friend of tax collectors and sinners!* Yet wisdom is vindicated by her deeds. (Matt 11:16-19)

Having just pondered the identity and role of both the Baptist and Jesus, this section highlights the response of the people to both figures sent by God, whilst incidentally giving us more information about Jesus' style of ministry and his priorities. Jesus refers to this generation, which is almost a technical term to describe his contemporaries. The pejorative term is rooted in the Old Testament, where it is applied to the people who were led by Moses through the wilderness, attached to such descriptors as *faithless, evil, sinful, perverse, crooked.*[64] The people of Jesus' time are seen to have much in common with the people of the time of Noah and of Moses.

Jesus is an acute observer of what happens around him. In the parable he uses on this occasion, he likens the people's responses to the Baptist and himself to what happens in the market place where children are sitting around and playing games. The structure of the brief parable is carefully orchestrated in parallels, a characteristic feature of Hebrew poetry: the piping and the refusal to dance; the wailing and the refusal to mourn. Similarly, the twofold application of the parable has a parallel structure: John does not eat or drink, inviting a critical response; Jesus eats and drinks, inviting a similar response. The overall structure takes a crossover or chiastic format: *joy, sorrow/sorrow, joy.*[65]

The precise nature of the game is unclear. It could be that one group of children is active and wants to play at weddings, but the other group refuses to join in. So the same active group then changes key and wishes to play at funerals, and again the others are unwilling to participate. Alternatively, one group is keen on playing at weddings, the other at funerals, and neither will budge. Yet another interpretation stresses the word *sitting.*[66] One group of children is sitting around and tries to get the others firstly to dance and then to mourn. The other group is non-cooperative, and the first cohort ridicules them as spoilsports.

There are different ways of interpreting the parable.[67] Some view the youngsters who are seated as representing this generation. They give orders and attempt to dictate the play and call the tune, demanding that John and then Jesus should fall in with their agendas and whims. In different ways both John and Jesus have been unwilling to accede to their demands, to modify or adapt their message and style of ministry; they have remained true to their vision of their mission.[68] Alternatively, others see the active children as representing Jesus and the Baptist respectively. Jesus calls for celebration and John for repentance. The people, this generation, ignore them both. In his presentation Jesus highlights the differences between the Baptist and himself. John was an ascetic, with a harsh and demanding lifestyle, an unusual appearance, and a message of repentance laced with threats of imminent fiery judgement. The people were critical, and labelled him as crazy, or, equivalently in that culture, as possessed by a devil, a comment was levelled also at Jesus on occasion.[69]

The people at the time preferred dancing and celebration. Jesus himself, on the other hand, comes along with a very different message and style. He emphasises God's compassion, acceptance and forgiveness. He enjoys a meal, is partial to a drink, and mixes freely in friendship with dishonest tax gatherers and sinners.[70] This causes raised eyebrows, strong criticism, deep scandal and rejection; dancing and celebration are jettisoned for puritanical mourning. It seems, then, that whatever kind of prophet God sends to his people, offering them a way to salvation, they are unwilling to respond positively; they are not prepared to welcome and to participate in what is being freely offered.

The final comment attributed to Jesus is rather obscure: *And yet wisdom is vindicated by her deeds.*[71] In the original statement *wisdom* probably refers to God's plan of salvation. Despite the rejection by Israel of God's final prophets, God's saving plan will finally win through. Matthew identifies Jesus with Wisdom. Despite the lack of response and apparent failure, in the end Jesus will be vindicated by his deeds, his works of healing and compassion, which demonstrate that God's Kingdom is now present. The responsibility for failure to recognise his identity and accept his message rests squarely with his contemporaries. *The compelling evidence of what Jesus has done is not impaired by the perversity of its reception.*[72]

Reflections

This parable of Jesus captures so vividly our human experience of finding ourselves in no-win situations. In marriage with our partner, in dealings with our children or ageing parents, in our workplaces, at times with our friends, in ministry and leadership, in games and sport, there are times when whatever we do is wrong. It can be so frustrating and so disheartening.

At least we can be aware that Jesus knows how we feel! Perhaps we need to make sure that we don't lose our sense of humour. Life can be like this! But it isn't always one-way traffic.

We all have the capacity to be spoilsports and wreckers, to withdraw our co-operation and sulk. When we catch ourselves playing this role, perhaps it's good to ask ourselves why, what is it about at a deeper level. If we are open and honest with ourselves, we can learn a lot about ourselves. And then we can do something to rectify our attitudes and behaviour, and be people who are positive, constructive and creatively optimistic.

Another tendency, which a certain understanding of the parable reveals, is the desire to control, to dictate what's going on, to call the tune, to impose on others, to get our own way, and then to complain bitterly when we don't succeed in our self-centred endeavours. Sometimes such tendencies can be executed with great subtlety and skill, sometimes with a certain bluff clumsiness. In any case, such behaviour betrays a lack of respect for the value and individuality and freedom of others.

In the context of the original parable the tragedy was that God's approach in love was being rejected. People had their own agendas and were closed to the wonderful gift on offer. They allowed their preconceived ideas, their expectations and prejudices to make them deaf to the message of salvation, blind to the expressions of God's saving presence in Jesus. They risked missing out on the most important and wonderful thing they could possibly experience. This Advent we need to ask ourselves whether we run a similar risk. We can get so caught up in our plans and projects, our busy lifestyles, our modern gadgets, that we are oblivious to the gentle presence of God in and around us.

The Baptist Again

The Baptist features again in the Gospel reading chosen for today. This time the context is different. The story has moved on. Matthew has already recounted the death of the Baptist in prison and his burial by his disciples. He includes the detail that the disciples had informed Jesus of what had taken place.[73] Since then Jesus has twice multiplied the loaves and fishes and fed the crowds, has healed many people, and has had conflicts with the religious leadership. Peter has professed his faith in Jesus' identity at Caesarea Philippi, and for the first time, to the consternation of his disciples, Jesus has spoken openly about his passion and death. Subsequently, Jesus was transfigured on the mountain in the company of Peter, James and John. As they are coming down from the mountain after this remarkable experience, Jesus enjoins that they should not tell anyone until the Son of Man has been raised from the dead.[74] At this juncture, realising from their recent experience that the new age has begun to dawn, they ask Jesus about Elijah, who had been present alongside Moses talking with Jesus during the vision on the mountain.

> And the disciples asked him, *Why, then, do the scribes say that Elijah must come first?* He replied, *Elijah is indeed coming and will restore all things; but I tell you that Elijah has already come, and they did not recognize him, but they did to him whatever they pleased. So also the Son of Man is about to suffer at their hands.* Then the disciples understood that he was speaking to them about John the Baptist. (Matt 17:10-13)

The disciples' question picks up the issue we have recently encountered concerning the relationship between Elijah, the Baptist and Jesus.[75]

The professional scribal and popular tradition was that Elijah would have a role in preparing for God's definitive intervention in salvation history.[76] He was expected to come again before the Day of the Lord, to act as forerunner either of the Messiah or of God's Kingdom. The disciples are puzzled that, if Jesus is the Messiah, this seems not to have happened. Jesus endorses the tradition of Elijah's coming and his work of renewal and restoration,[77] but goes on to state categorically his own conviction (*I tell you*) that Elijah has in fact already come. However, the people failed to recognise him and to believe, and treated him badly. The disciples realise that he is identifying the Baptist with Elijah's role, something which he had done to the crowds earlier.[78] The correct appraisal of the Baptist further clarifies the identity of Jesus.

Jesus then returns to what he has recently stated to his disciples at Caesarea Philippi. In the light of the transfiguration experience which they have witnessed, his words are particularly relevant. Just as the Baptist suffered and was executed, so Jesus, the Son of Man, will suffer a similar fate at the hands of his people. It is clear that the idea which the disciples may have about the kind of Messiah they wish Jesus to be will need radical readjustment; the concept of a suffering Messiah and its implications for discipleship do not resonate comfortably with them. They have glimpsed his glory, but such glory will not come about until after he has suffered. The voice from the cloud engulfing the mountaintop urged them: *Listen to him.* As Jesus' story continues to unfold, it will become increasingly evident that on this topic the disciples find listening to his repeated warnings particularly difficult.

Reflections

In the Advent build up to the celebration of Christmas we generally sense something of the joy of that Feast. There are beautiful carol services and Christmas plays, and we catch the excitement of the youngsters. Today's Gospel reading, with its emphasis on failure, unbelief and violent response, tends to jar with all this.

Whilst it is true that God's love is shown so powerfully and gently in the swaddled child of Bethlehem, it is also true that the grown child will show his love by absorbing criticism, opposition and rejection, and finally submitting to a brutal and shameful death. That is the awful and awesome reality.

We know too that the preparation and actual celebration of Christmas can be a period of anxiety and stress, of loneliness and acute pain, and of strained relationships. That too is part of love and part of life. And the challenge which the contemporaries of Jesus faced lingers on and touches us today. Advent is a time when we are invited to ask ourselves just how fully we believe in Jesus and welcome him into our thinking and planning and living, so that his presence in our world and in our lives really does make a difference and actually fashions who we are. We may be aware of elements of unbelief, discomfort, and rejection in our own response to Jesus centuries later. It is important that we don't allow the paraphernalia of Christmas to obscure its real significance.

Endnotes

1. I have discussed Mark in *Jesus and the Little People* (Bolton, Don Bosco Publications 2012), p.49-55.
2. The *Pharisees* (separated ones) were deeply religious men who observed the Law and oral tradition strictly, especially in matters of ritual purity. They kept their distance from other people and were the defenders of strict Jewish orthodoxy. *The teachers of the Law*, often referred to as the *scribes*, were the professional interpreters of the Law; they were both theologians and lawyers; most of them were Pharisees.
3. Green, p.240, observes that in Luke the *power of the Lord* is equivalent to the *Spirit of the Lord*.
4. In Mark the roof would probably have consisted of branches and hardened mud. Luke seems to have a Roman-type house in mind, though Marshall, p.213, suggests that tiled roofs were in use in Palestine by this time.
5. This is the first mention of *faith* in the Gospel; for Johnson, p.93, it denotes hope, trust and perseverance.
6. Green, p.241. As *Son of Man* (Jesus' favourite self-designation) he has delegated authority; also Caird, p.94.
7. The ability to perceive inner thoughts and attitudes is typical of a prophet (see Byrne, p.59). As Simeon states (2:35) *the thoughts of many will be revealed.* Jesus is also bypassing the normal Temple system with regard to forgiveness.
8. In using the term *readership* I am not unaware that originally the Gospel was proclaimed rather than read. For a fascinating discussion of this, see Whitney Shiner, *Proclaiming the Gospel: first century performance of Mark* (Harrisburg, Trinity Press International 2003).
9. Meier, *Matthew*, p.199, calls the section (18:1-35) *Church Life and Order*; Byrne, p.139, *Life in the Community of the Church*. This is the fourth of the five major discourses of the Gospel. The evangelist is responsible for bringing together sayings of Jesus of disparate origin into a connected format usually called a *discourse*. Some sayings are found in Mark, others in

the Q source, and some only in Matthew. (See Senior, p.204).

10. Many commentators follow this bi-partite division with sub-sections (see Beare, p.373; Harrington, p.265; Byrne, p.140-143).

11. Matthew has adapted the dispute of Mark 9:24, 33-37, and thereby he improves the disciples' image, as is his wont. Perhaps there is a link with the recent emphasis on Peter's role. The preoccupation with power recurs in 20:20-28.

12. Harrington, p.266. Meier, *Matthew*, p.201 describes children as *pieces of property without any rights; powerless to defend themselves, they had to rely totally on others.* Wright, 2:27, suggests that the child was a girl, because that would make Jesus' point most effectively, *that the weakest, most vulnerable, least significant human being you can think of is the clearest possible signpost to what the Kingdom of God will be like.*

13. See Hagner, p.518. Harrington, p.266, notes that the disciples' concern with greatness fits comfortably into first century Judaism; the Qumran community, for instance, was very highly structured.

14. In 19:13-15 Jesus, contrary to the wishes of his disciples, insists on receiving and blessing the children brought to him.

15. Byrne, p.140.

16. Hagner, p.520; Beare, p.376. Jesus could well have had a wider application in mind.

17. Davies & Allison, p.301. Hagner, p.527, notes that *the security of the remaining ninety nine while the shepherd is absent is not a matter of concern in the parable.* Ezek 34:15-16 provides some background: *I will seek the lost and I will bring back the strayed.*

18. Green, p.162; Hagner, p.525; Harrington, p.265.

19. Davies & Allison, p.301; also Hagner, p.527. In Matthew, as we have seen, Jesus is referred to several times as shepherd (9:36; 15:24; 26:31).

20. Byrne, p.141; Davies & Allison, p.299.

21. Senior, p.208, understands that Jesus' words are addressed to pastoral leaders rather than the community as a whole, whereas Schweizer, p.369, maintains that the parable challenges the whole community.

22. Hagner, p.322.

23. Schweizer, p.272.
24. Byrne, p.96.
25. Hill, p.207, notes that this legalism becomes evident in the following chapter of controversies.
26. 23:4; see Acts 15:10.
27. See 28:19.
28. The two terms are practically interchangeable in meaning: thus Harrington, p.168. Moses is referred to as *meek* in Num 12:3; *meek and humble* are found together in Jer 26:6 and Zeph 3:2. Paul in 2 Cor 10:4 refers to Jesus in these terms. The Pharisees are criticised in 23:5-12 for their arrogance.
29. 12:15-21; 21:5; he proclaims the meek blessed in 5:3.
30. Meier, *Matthew*, p.128.
31. Exod 33:14. Davies & Allison, p.187, note that the messianic age was to be a time of rest, like a great Sabbath. The eschatology is *realised* or present. See also Byrne, p.96.
32. 6:16. Green, p.122, points out that in Jeremiah the people, sadly, decide not to walk in that way. This therefore points forward to Jesus' later rejection.
33. Sir 51:23-26; thus Senior, p.133; Hagner, p.323; Beare, p.267; Albright & Mann, p.146; Green, p.122. Harrington, p.170, sees Sirach as a kind of advertisement for a school; so Jesus is using the language of teachers in a wisdom school.
34. Hagner, p.323.
35. Byrne, p.97.
36. Davies & Allison, p.188.
37. 5:20; see, for instance, Byrne p.97.
38. Byrne, p.97.
39. Byrne, p.98.
40. For a brief discussion of the Baptist see *Jesus and the Little People*, p.12-16; for a more thorough treatment see Meier, *Marginal*, 1:16-177.
41. This discourse (10:5-42) is the second of Matthew's five. Harrington, p.158, maintains that three originally unconnected topics concerning the relationship between Jesus and the Baptist were brought together in the Q source (see the parallel in Luke 7:18-35).

42. Matthew gives no indication of the place where the Baptist is held; we are dependent on the contemporary Jewish historian Josephus for this additional information. The Baptist's later martyrdom is recounted in 14:1-12.

43. Hagner, p.300, notes that he has heard of the *works of the Christ*, (the works which the Messiah was expected to perform), but was unsure whether Jesus was in fact that figure.

44. 3:11

45. Traditionally, it has been claimed that John's question was asked primarily for the sake of his disciples. This is a view which contemporary scholarship would question; see Meier, 2:132-137. Green, p.114, believes that the question is asked in the name of the old Israel.

46. Isa 26:19; 29:18; 35:5-6; 42:7,18; 61:1. Hagner, p.301, observes that these passages refer to the anticipated messianic era. Jesus in Matt 5:3 refers to the poor who possess the Kingdom.

47. The blind in 9:27-31; the lame in 9:2-8; the lepers in 8:1-4; the deaf in 8:32-33; the dead in 9:18-26; the preaching to the poor in 4:23; 9:35. Note the careful correlation; this passage provides an interpretation of chapters 4-10.

48. This will happen to his family (12:46), in Nazareth (13:57), according to the parable of the sower (13:21), and with the Pharisees (15:12). At the Last Supper Jesus predicts that the disciples will be scandalised too (26:31,33). The ultimate stumbling block or obstacle to faith is the crucifixion (1 Cor1:23).

49. Harrington, p.159, suggests a view which understands Jesus' words as a reinterpretation of the Jewish messianic expectations of the day. He also points out that there was no uniform or dominant idea of the messiah in first-century Judaism. In the Psalms of Solomon (1st century BC) the future descendant of David will be a political and military leader, ridding Jerusalem of its Gentile conquerors. Perhaps Jesus is reacting also against this kind of expectation.

50. Meier, *Matthew*, p.120.

51. Jesus actually says *go out into the wilderness*. According to

Meier, *Marginal*, 2:139, the lower part of the Jordan river was close to the Judean desert, and was often referred to as *wilderness*. The reed also might imply the reed symbol on coins minted by Herod in AD 19 on the occasion of the founding of the lakeside city of Tiberias.

52. Senior, p.127.
53. This is a mixed quotation using Exod 23:20LXX and Mal 3:1. Mark uses this quotation at the outset of his Gospel in 1:2, and Matthew omits it at that point. Meier, *Marginal*, 2:141, considers the quotation as probably a Christian composition added to an authentic saying of Jesus about the Baptist.
54. Davies & Allison, p.177; Byrne, p.92-93.
55. Beare, p.259-260, envisages much of this as a dialogue between Matthew's Church and disciples of the Baptist who are active in the vicinity.
56. Byrne, p.93. Senior, p.125, notes that Luke 7:24-28 contains parallel words concerning the Baptist's place in salvation history, but not the saying about violence. It is found in a different context and with a different meaning in Luke 16:16.
57. John himself did not proclaim the Kingdom.
58. Hagner, p.307; Beare, p.260. Davies & Allison, p.178, link the idea with the expectation of eschatological tribulation. Such opposition has also been experienced by Matthew's Church.
59. Byrne, p.93 fn4, using the Greek middle voice rather than the passive for biazetai. Similarly, as a possibility, Meier, *Matthew*, p.122. Others disagree; for example Albright and Mann, p.137; Green, p.116; Hill, p.200-201, who suggests that Luke's version may be open to this interpretation.
60. Harrington, p.157, notes the debate as to whether Jewish tradition expected Elijah to be forerunner of the Messiah or of God's Kingdom. On p.161 he suggests the possibility that the idea of John's role as Elijah preparing the way for the Messiah was a Christian adaptation of Mal 4:5-6. Meier, *Marginal*, 2:156, maintains that the affirmation that John is Elijah is Matthaean redaction.
61. Matthew's word order, *all the prophets and the law*, is unique, as he creatively understands the law as integral to the prophetic tradition.

62. 17:12
63. Meier, *Marginal*, 2:136.
64. Deut 1:35; 32:5,20. Jesus adopts this phrase in a number of situations.
65. Meier, *Marginal*, 2:147-148.
66. Jeremias, *The Parables of Jesus* (London, SCM 1972), p.160-162.
67. See Davies & Allison, p.180; Meier, *Matthew*, p.123; Green, p.117.
68. Jeremias, p.160-162; Meier, *Marginal*, 2:148.
69. Mark 3:21
70. This description of Jesus recalls the Old Testament description of the rebellious son who leads people astray and should be stoned to death (Deut 21:18-21). See Wright, 1,132; Jeremias, p.160.
71. Luke 7:35 has *by all her children*. On this see Meier, *Marginal*, 2:153. Scholars maintain that Luke is probably nearer the original.
72. Green, p.118.
73. 14:1-12
74. There are hints of Moses coming down from Sinai (Exod 34:29LXX). Several times in the Gospel narrative Jesus enjoins silence concerning his identity, lest it be misunderstood.
75. The reading for *Thursday*.
76. Mal 4:5-6LXX *Behold I will send you Elijah the prophet before the great and terrible day of the Lord comes*; also 3:1; Sir 48:10.
77. Davies & Allison, p.285, note that the future tense (*will restore*) agrees simply with what the scribes and Old Testament say.
78. 11:14. Matthew is the only NT writer to equate Elijah and John explicitly. For Matthew these verses provide an answer to Jewish criticisms of Christian claims in his own day.

The lectionary provides readings for five days during the third week of Advent, Monday to Friday, and another series of readings to begin on December 17th. Since the date of the first Sunday of Advent is variable, these take priority if there is an overlap.

Week Three

A Matter of Authority

We remain with Matthew for today's Gospel reading, but the story of Jesus has moved on apace. Jesus has made the journey up to the city of Jerusalem with his disciples and other pilgrims in order to celebrate the feast of Passover. He has entered the city in a solemn fashion, an entry which has caused considerable turmoil amongst the locals. In response to their question about his identity, those accompanying Jesus said: *This is the prophet Jesus from Nazareth in Galilee.* Once within the confines of the city, Jesus headed to the Temple and drove out those involved in trading,[1] stating, *It is written My house shall be called a house of prayer, but you are making it a den of robbers.* Jesus then spent the night in Bethany, and in the morning made the journey from there back into the city, cursing the barren fig tree en route. Once again he makes his way into the Temple.

When he entered the temple, the chief priests and the elders of the people came to him as he was teaching, and said, *By what authority are you doing these things, and who gave you this authority?* Jesus said to them, *I will also ask you one question; if you tell me the answer, then I will also tell you by what authority I do these things. Did the baptism of John come from heaven, or was it of human origin?* And they argued with one another, *If we say, "From heaven", he will say to us, "Why then did you not believe him?" But if we say, "Of human origin", we are afraid of the crowd; for all regard John as a prophet.* So they answered Jesus, *We do not know.* And he said to them, *Neither will I tell you by what authority I am doing these things.* (Matt 21:23-27)

On returning to the Temple, Jesus immediately begins to teach the people there, probably about the coming of the Kingdom.[2]

He is approached by the local religious elite, the power brokers of Jerusalem.[3] Their problem is doubtless prompted by his actions the previous day in making a solemn entry into the city, and then engaging in an overt prophetic critique of the Temple system. But the issue of Jesus' authority is one which has frequently erupted in Galilee too as Jesus' ministry has unfolded. The representatives of the Sanhedrin are not seeking information; their aggressive and cunning question is designed to entice Jesus into claiming openly that he is the Messiah and that his authority comes from God, in this way providing them with evidence which would enable them to accuse him of blasphemy.[4] Jesus refuses to answer them directly, and replies in rabbinic style by posing a counterquestion. Again it is the role of the Baptist which is the topic. Jesus challenges them to articulate publically their view about the origin of his baptism, whether it came from heaven, from God, or whether it was simply a human invention.

Jesus' adversaries are thrown into confusion by his clever question which catapults them onto the horns of a dilemma. They are not slow to recognise that he has cornered them. They are well aware that the people have a high regard for the Baptist, considering him as a prophet from God.[5] To deny that would be to court disaster. They themselves have been unwilling to acknowledge and welcome him in that way, for he clearly had little regard for the Temple and its corrupt system, and his call for radical conversion was uncompromising. His mission bypassed them as people who were no longer relevant in God's designs.

In the end they opt for expediency and decline to answer the question, rather tamely asserting that they do not know. In the absence of spin doctors, they brazenly refuse to be drawn, their shallowness exposed, their own competence and authority, as religious leaders, eroded. *We do not know.* But the question which Jesus asked, though ostensibly about the Baptist, was equally relevant concerning his own position. If he was from God, he had God's authority for his actions. They had already made up their minds that that could not be the case; its implications would be devastating for them.

Their decision about Jesus will shortly become chillingly evident as they will be the principal instigators of the process which leads to his death.[6] Their refusal to believe the Baptist is mirrored in their attitude to Jesus. There is continuity between the two. They are totally closed to Jesus, deaf to his message. At this point, in the light of their evasive choice, Jesus is content to play the same game, refusing to answer their question. *His refusal is in fact veiled affirmation.*[7] But his challenge remains.

Reflections

Jesus is not afraid to challenge the system when it is unfit for purpose, and to take on those in power when they have lost sight of God's presence and rejected God's way. The history of the Church is replete with individuals who have been moved to follow his lead with courage and integrity. Some have challenged aspects of Church life, others have stood up to political oppression. All of us are called through baptism to embrace prophetic responsibility, uncomfortable though it can be. Often we prefer to close our eyes and ears, and leave the challenging role to others: playing it safe. And so evils blossom, people continue to suffer, the coming of the Kingdom is further delayed. Perhaps today we could question ourselves about these tendencies.

The religious elite in today's episode cut a sorry figure. Genuinely perturbed by Jesus' words and actions, desperate to maintain their power base, they have recourse to cunning and insincerity in order to trap him. Rocked onto the back foot by his clever counterquestion, their true colours exposed, they lose credibility. We all bridle when we encounter insincerity, double-dealing, evasion or manipulation. Integrity, uprightness and truthfulness can at times seem hard to come by. Advent furnishes an opportunity for us to examine our own lives and to ask whether we are not in some ways caught up in this kind of behaviour, whether we are compromised sometimes by what we say or do, and by our silence. The honesty and courage of Jesus offers an alternative, though potentially dangerous, way.

Yes & No

The Gospel reading for today follows on directly from that which we considered yesterday.

What do you think? A man had two sons; he went to the first and said, "Son, go and work in the vineyard today." He answered, "I will not"; but later he changed his mind and went. The father went to the second and said the same; and he answered, "I go, sir"; but he did not go. Which of the two did the will of his father? They said, *The first.* Jesus said to them, *Truly I tell you, the tax collectors and the prostitutes are going into the kingdom of God ahead of you. For John came to you in the way of righteousness and you did not believe him, but the tax collectors and the prostitutes believed him; and even after you saw it, you did not change your minds and believe him.* (Matt 21:28-32)

Jesus is still in the Temple precincts after his initial bruising encounter with the religious leaders. The context is still one of controversy, for they remain the principal audience as Jesus continues to teach the people gathered there. His teaching now takes the form of a trilogy of parables: the parable of the two sons, the parable of the wicked tenants, and the parable of the wedding banquet. In the first of these, found only in Matthew,[8] the Advent figure of the Baptist is again mentioned, as a link is forged with the preceding story.

Jesus, an accomplished teacher, engages his audience with a question, which is rhetorical: *What do you think?* He then presents a homely scenario. A father with two sons asks each in turn to go and do some work in tending the vineyard.[9] He addresses the first, probably the elder, affectionately as *Son*.

Surprisingly, he responds with a blunt refusal: *I will not.* Such disobedience is culturally unacceptable. But later he has a change of mind and heart, and goes along to carry out his father's request. By contrast, the other son shows great respect to his father, addressing him as *Sir*, and immediately promises to do his bidding. *I go, sir.* But he has no intention of complying; there is no mention of his changing his mind; his words are empty.[10] Jesus puts a second question to his audience: *Which of the two did the will of his father?* And they are obliged to provide the correct, but incriminating answer: *The first.*

In itself, the parable could have originally been a defence of Jesus' ministry to the outcasts and sinners in the face of criticism from the religious elite. It could also illustrate the split between saying and doing which often occurs in our lives.[11] However, with the application which Jesus here provides, the parable continues the polemic against the religious authorities. Jesus shocks them by identifying them as actors in the parable drama. Mention of a vineyard may symbolically represent Israel.[12] The tax collectors and prostitutes, who are despised and banished to the religious periphery, are in fact now entering God's Kingdom first. Initially, their lifestyle suggested a refusal to obey God's will as expressed in the Law. When the Baptist came, however, these were the ones who responded positively to his message. The religious leaders, highly respected and powerful men, expert in the requirements of the Law, initially refused to believe in John, the prophet sent by God, refused to accept his invitation to conversion, and, unlike the first son, did not change their mind even when they saw the radical change in the lives of those viewed as *sinners*. The way of righteousness has to do with responding generously to God's approach and demands, by a change of mind, heart and lifestyle, and so fulfilling God's will.

What was true of the Baptist is true of Jesus. Those on the margins of organised religion, those considered *sinners* by the religious elite, have been the ones who have responded to Jesus' approach, his message, his openness and compassion. They have welcomed the inbreak of the Kingdom.

Those who felt comfortable and secure in their traditional religiosity, however, especially the leaders, have been unwilling to move out of their normal parameters into the new reality which Jesus is introducing.[13] Entering the Kingdom *before you* may really mean *instead of you*.[14] The leaders of Israel in Jesus' day continue the tradition of rejecting the prophets sent to them by God.

Reflections

In this parable it is not difficult for us to identity with the three characters. As parents, pastors, educators, we have all been in the position of asking others to do something. Sometimes the response has been a refusal, and this is hard to take. We feel disappointed, hurt, let down, rejected, angry – a whole gamut of emotions. A transformation, like a mini-resurrection, occurs when the individual changes his/her mind and fulfils our request. Sometimes the response to our request has seemed like an enthusiastic or generous *Yes*, that wonderful little word of acceptance, empathy, cooperation. This makes us feel good, maybe relieves some anxiety or hesitation. And then there follows the shock of realising that the *Yes* has come to nothing, and we experience another range of emotions.

Looking back on our lives we may recall occasions when we have been the ones to refuse to do what has been asked of us. We have probably felt that the request was unfair or unreasonable, too demanding, inconvenient. But later, we've thought better of it and decided to abandon our negativity and our upset feelings, and carry out the request made of us. Sometimes the acceptance has been rather grudging, sometimes more generous. Or perhaps we are aware of occasions when we have agreed for peace in the house, for a quiet life, to humour someone, and our response has not been genuine and sincere. We have gone away and neglected to keep our word.

Advent gives us an opportunity to think about the way we respond to requests made of us and the way in which we treat those who ask.

But Advent also challenges us to extrapolate a little and consider our response to God. This was the issue for Jesus in telling this parable. Perhaps in the past we have at times uttered an outright *No* to God's approach and God's demands, but then repented, changed mind and heart, and responded with love. As Advent progresses, perhaps we need to make time and space to listen carefully for what God is asking of us today – through the words of scripture, through other people, through situations which crop up, through the world around us, through the longings deep in our hearts.

Advent also invites us to ponder whether we are prone to simply go through the motions of discipleship. We say a kind of *Yes* to God but somehow don't quite get round to doing what is required. We procrastinate, manufacture flimsy excuses, develop avoidance techniques, effectively turning our *Yes* into a *No*. We are missing or wasting opportunities for growth, for generosity, for unselfishness. We are keeping God at a safe distance, and are only half alive, if that.

In Matthew's Gospel, Jesus several times stresses the importance of action rather than words. It is not the one who repeatedly invokes the Lord who will enter the Kingdom of Heaven, *but the one who does the will of my Father in heaven.*[15] The wise man who builds his house on a rock is one, *who hears these words of mine and acts on them.*[16] Those who do the heavenly Father's will become the brothers, sisters and mother of Jesus.[17] In the parable of the Judgement, the emphasis in Jesus' words is on action which expresses care and concern for those in need. Perhaps the parable also shows that God looks to the final outcome of our lives. God can put up with an initial *No*, and a lot of other *No's* besides, on the way to a final and lasting *Yes*.[18] And there is always the danger that the righteous, who appear to be religious and observant, should fail to understand the immense compassionate love and mercy of God, whereas those aware of their weakness and need can be open to God's free gift of the Kingdom.

The Coming One

The Gospel reading chosen for today is Luke's version of the passage from Matthew which we considered last week as an introduction to Thursday's reading. *The disciples of John reported all these things to him. So John summoned two of his disciples and sent them to the Lord to ask, Are you the one who is to come, or are we to wait for another? When the men had come to him, they said, John the Baptist has sent us to you to ask, "Are you the one who is to come, or are we to wait for another?" Jesus had just then cured many people of diseases, plagues, and evil spirits, and had given sight to many who were blind. And he answered them, Go and tell John what you have seen and heard: the blind receive their sight, the lame walk, the lepers are cleansed, the deaf hear, the dead are raised, the poor have good news brought to them. And blessed is anyone who takes no offence at me.* (Luke 7: 19-23)

Luke, after presenting Jesus' sermon on the plain,[19] describes the healing of the Gentile centurion's slave at Capernaum. Jesus then moves on to the town of Nain, where he shows great compassion to the widow whose only son has died, by restoring him to life.[20] The response of the people who have witnessed what has happened is: *A great prophet has arisen among us... God has looked favourably on his people.*

It is implied that the disciples of John the Baptist have been present, and so have gleaned a great deal of information to communicate to their Master, now in prison, concerning what Jesus has been saying and doing, and the way in which people are responding to him.[21] It is clear that there is a discrepancy between the style and outlook of the Baptist and that of Jesus.

Earlier in the story the reader is informed about the preaching of the Baptist near the Jordan, in which he refers to, *The wrath to come, and the axe lying at the root of the trees.* As the precursor, he describes the one coming after him as baptising, not with water like him, but with the Holy Spirit and fire. *His winnowing fork is in his hand, to clear the threshing floor and to gather the wheat into his granary; but the chaff he will burn with unquenchable fire.*[22] John is expecting imminent judgement; the overthrowing of wrong. The tone and emphasis in the words of Jesus are different, as is evident in his inaugural sermon in Nazareth.[23] The activities he is engaged in, healing and exorcising, are also different. This puzzles the Baptist and spurs him to seek clarification as to whether Jesus is the figure he envisaged. So he sends two of his disciples[24] to put the crucial question concerning Jesus' identity in blunt terms: *Are you the one who is to come, or are we to wait for another?* Two was the normally accepted number for genuine witnesses. The disciples do what they have been asked to do, repeating John's question verbatim.

In the meantime, Jesus has been continuing his healing activity, and so in answer, rather than a simple *Yes* or *No*, he points his visitors to what has been happening and what they themselves have witnessed: blind people see, the lame can now walk, lepers are cleansed, those who were deaf can hear again, the dead are raised to life. These phrases strongly echo the messianic expectations of the prophet Isaiah.[25] The evidence is clear and points to the presence of the promised eschatological salvation. And he adds in the place of emphasis that the poor and ordinary people have been brought Good News. His final comment, while couched in general terms, is something of a challenge to his interlocutors: *Blessed is anyone who has taken no offence at me.* Jesus is aware John is struggling to come to terms with the unexpected style of his ministry; he is sensitive to his perplexity.[26] The messengers are left to draw their own conclusions and report back.[27]

The response of Jesus throws the burden of discernment back to the Baptist. One issue is to clarify the kind of *coming one* he was expecting or hoping for. If the message and activities of Jesus measure up, the Baptist has his answer: *he need not wait for another.* If there is a discrepancy, Jesus indirectly invites him to think again before dismissing him, and not be put off by his quite different approach and style. The prophecies really are being fulfilled.

Reflections

In this passage we find a deeply religious and committed man in a state of some confusion and perplexity. He has very clear ideas about God and God's ways. The arrival of Jesus on the scene with different priorities and a different agenda has thrown him into turmoil. He needs and seeks clarification. Perhaps we can identify with him to some extent. The arrival of Pope Francis into the Vatican has created for many of our contemporaries a similar experience of uncertainty. Long established ways and styles and systems have been gently but strongly challenged. This kind of thing can happen to all of us less dramatically on a regular basis. We are called to reassess our priorities, examine our values.

One writer says: *Another attractive facet in the personality of Jesus is seen in his dealings with John the Baptist. In spite of the deep gulf that separated his radiant friendliness from John's forbidding austerity, he had a profound appreciation of his grim herald.*[28] By means of John's emissaries, Jesus lays before him the evidence; evidence with a solid scriptural pedigree. In a gentle way Jesus is showing John that some of his expectations need to be revised quite radically; only then will he be able to answer his own questioning. With us that is often the case too. We can create expectations of ourselves, our loved ones, those for whom we work. We need a reality check, a motivation check; we need to evaluate evidence dispassionately; we need the freedom to adapt, to change and to move forward.

Advent provides a wonderful opportunity to see whether we are securely grounded or building castles in the air. Jesus has a deep appreciation for each of us, but he may want us to be alert and sensitive enough to discern the need for modification, perhaps even a radical reappraisal and change of direction.

Reeds, Fashion & Greatness

The Gospel reading for today flows directly from yesterday's episode. After the visit of the Baptist's disciples, with the question from their Master, they return to him conveying Jesus' answer. In their absence the narrative moves on.

When John's messengers had gone, Jesus began to speak to the crowds about John: *What did you go out into the wilderness to look at? A reed shaken by the wind? What then did you go out to see? Someone dressed in soft robes? Look, those who put on fine clothing and live in luxury are in royal palaces. What then did you go out to see? A prophet? Yes, I tell you, and more than a prophet. This is the one about whom it is written,*

"See, I am sending my messenger ahead of you, who will prepare your way before you."

I tell you, among those born of women no one is greater than John; yet the least in the kingdom of God is greater than he. (And all the people who heard this, including the tax collectors, acknowledged the justice of God, because they had been baptized with John's baptism. But by refusing to be baptized by him, the Pharisees and the lawyers rejected God's purpose for themselves.) (Luke 7:24-30)

Again we have here Luke's version of the words of Jesus which we have already encountered in Matthew's Gospel. Jesus picks up the issue of the Baptist's identity and role. He recalls the way in which the crowds went out into the wilderness by the Jordan River to encounter John.[29] The reeds by the riverside, being blown about by the wind, have little to offer, nor are they an accurate reflection of the Baptist, who was not wavering or uncertain. Nor was he the kind of person dressed in fine clothing and living in luxury.

He was known to be an ascetic. What they were interested in was to meet a prophet, a man of strength and conviction,[30] a person who proclaims the word of God. In this their estimation was correct. But Jesus goes on to assert even more. Quoting Malachi he presents the Baptist as the one sent by God to prepare the way for the *coming one*.[31]

The final statement of Jesus is challenging. No one who has ever been born is greater than he – amazing praise indeed.[32] However, *That to which John's ministry pointed and for which it prepared has broken into the world, so that conventional ways of measuring honour and status have been inverted.*[33] The least of those who are already in the Kingdom have greater standing than he. The distinction between old and new reality, promise and fulfilment, is telling. The Baptist, for all his importance, belongs to the past era.[34]

The evangelist concludes with a parenthesis, observing that many of Jesus' listeners, some of whom were even tax collectors, had recognised John as a prophet from God and received John's baptism, and on hearing Jesus, praised God. Such people are open to Jesus too. The religious elite, on the other hand, who rejected him, are rejecting God's saving purpose – a strong statement.[35] What was true for John is true for Jesus.

Reflections

In his questions Jesus offers us three interesting lines of thought. Are we like reeds swaying to and fro in the wind, unstable, fickle, lacking consistency or conviction? Is our lifestyle one of indulgence, soft and superficial, self-centred and materialistic? Or are we prophetic people, living with conviction, integrity and simplicity, God-centred and genuine, reliable and true? It is so easy for us to get caught up in the values of the world around us, values which paradoxically get highlighted in the Advent build-up to Christmas when consumerism can run rampant, and balance, serenity and peace can melt away, and our true focus becomes blurred. Swimming against the tide is never easy. And yet the following of Jesus so often demands precisely that.

For all his goodness and commitment to God, the Baptist belonged to the past. He had a God-sent role, but it had been superseded by the coming of Jesus. He was struggling with the need to let go, change his vision, and accept a different way of understanding God. The originality and deep humanity of Jesus, his closeness to the marginalised and *sinners*, was hard to take. I believe that there is still so much about the Gospel of Jesus that is disconcerting for all of us, even though we seek to be his disciples. For all his kindness and love, he can be an irritant, disturbing and unsettling us. At times we too can be perplexed and confused by it all, and left wondering. Advent provides us with the opportunity to reflect about this.

On Testimony

The final reading prior to the Infancy Narrative material set in place from December 17th is taken from the Gospel of John.[36] This is the only passage in Advent from the Fourth Gospel, and its selection seems to be motivated by the mention of the Baptist. Jesus is addressing his opponent.

> You sent messengers to John, and he testified to the truth. Not that I accept such human testimony, but I say these things so that you may be saved. He was a burning and shining lamp, and you were willing to rejoice for a while in his light. But I have a testimony greater than John's. The works that the Father has given me to complete, the very works that I am doing, testify on my behalf that the Father has sent me. (John 5: 33-36)

The focus in chapters 2-4 of John's Gospel is on different faith responses to Jesus. The emphasis in chapters 5-10 is about the relationship of Jesus to the Jewish festivals: Sabbath, Passover, Tabernacles and Dedication. These Jesus brings to fulfilment and replaces. This sequence opens with Jesus curing a man by the side of the Bethesda pool in Jerusalem. The man inadvisedly reports what has happened to the religious leaders, who take umbrage because Jesus has healed him on a Sabbath day, and has therefore broken the law. The text reads that the Jews started persecuting Jesus because he was doing such things on the Sabbath. The Greek verb here translated as *persecute, give a hard time*, can also be rendered as *prosecute*. It can therefore have a forensic flavour. In fact, the rest of chapter five is cast as a kind of trial of Jesus.

It was commonly held in religious circles that God rested on the Sabbath except for two things: since children were born and people died on the Sabbath, God gave life and judged on the Sabbath. Jesus claims to have been given these prerogatives by God, his Father.

The Son gives life to whoever he wishes. The Father judges no one but has given all judgement to the Son. (John 5:21-22) As he continues speaking, Jesus brings forward a number of witnesses to testify on his behalf: the Baptist, his own works, the Father, the scriptures, Moses – quite a formidable array. We, the readers, enter the courtroom as this list begins.

The Prologue, with which the Fourth Gospel begins, states:
There was a man sent from God, whose name was John. He came as a witness to testify to the light, so that all might believe through him. He himself was not the light, but he came to testify to the light. The true light, which enlightens everyone, was coming into the world.[37]

As the Gospel proper opens, the Jews sent priests and Levites from Jerusalem, an official delegation, to ask him who he was. He gave testimony that he was not the Messiah, nor Elijah, nor the expected prophet. Rather, quoting Isaiah, he claimed to be the voice of one crying in the wilderness *Make straight the way of the Lord.* (John 1:23) His visitors, sent by the Pharisees, continued to interrogate him, asking him why, in that case, he was baptising. In reply, John states: *I baptise with water. Among you stands one whom you do not know, the one who is coming after me; I am not worthy to untie the thong of his sandal.* John soon afterwards testifies that Jesus is, *the Lamb of God who takes away the sin of the world.* He claims that he saw the Spirit come down on him and rest on him, and finally he testifies that, *This is the Son of God.*

In the Fourth Gospel John's primary role is the bear witness, and this is what he does. Jesus describes him as a lamp, burning and shining, who for a while attracted people who were delighted with his presence and basked in the glow of his light. But he is not the world's genuine light. True though his witness is, Jesus does not depend on human testimony. A more powerful and impressive witness is provided by the works which Jesus does.

In an earlier statement during the episode of Jesus' encounter with the Samaritan woman by the well of Sychar, when his disciples have returned with food after their shopping expedition and encourage Jesus to eat, Jesus says: *My food is to do the will of the one who sent me, and to complete his work*.[38] This is such a powerful expression of the unwavering focus of his life. This is what sustains him. His mission is profoundly oriented to the Father. It is the Father's will which Jesus is bent on doing, the Father's task, commission or work which he is committed to fulfil. The verb here translated as *complete* means to bring to final accomplishment, perfection, consummation.

This time Jesus again speaks of the works which have been entrusted to him, and which he must accomplish. The plural refers to his actions during his ministry which bring life to people, like his reaching out to bring healing to the man at the pool, who had been ill for thirty eight years. The things which Jesus says and does are part of the *work* given by the Father, which he must bring to accomplishment.[39] In these words, the one who sent him is rendered explicit; it is the Father's plan or design that is behind all that Jesus is and does. The Father sets the agenda. The work given by the Father to Jesus will finally be accomplished when Jesus has been lifted up on the cross on Calvary after another trial, the Sanhedrin session at which Caiaphas condemned him. Jesus' final words from the cross are, *It is finished.*

Reflections

This reading invites us to pick up the idea of light. Jesus comes to us as the light of our world. The imagery of light brightens our Christmas. Elsewhere Jesus tells his followers that we are the light of the world, and that our light needs to shine forth in witness to God's presence and God's love. There is such a great need in today's secularist and consumer-driven world for us to bear witness to a different set of values, a different understanding of what really matters in life. As Christians we are in a sense on trial. People can be quick to find fault, point the finger and criticise. They are not interested in the light we may shed. The message of Jesus, the values he lived by, can be a disturbing threat.

Like Jesus we have a work to accomplish, a mission to fulfil. Basically it is, like his mission, to reveal and make present the overwhelming love of the Father. And this happens through many works, as we seek to discern what love is demanding in all kinds of daily situations, and seek to respond lovingly with kindness, creativity and compassion. It is wonderful to know that, for all our weakness and fragility, we are caught up in the love of God, called to bear witness to God's presence and transforming power at all levels of life and in all circumstances, for every aspect of our experience is a facet of that overall experience. Advent can enable us to rediscover all this once again, to refocus, to embrace our mission, and cry, *Yes*.

Endnotes

1. For a fuller treatment, see Winstanley, *Lenten Sundays*, p.70-77. The trading was, of course, sanctioned by the religious leaders.
2. Hagner, p.609.
3. The Romans occupied and controlled Judea, but delegated ordinary business to the religious leaders, under the leadership of Caiaphas, the High Priest. This is the first of several conflict stories (five in number) and parables (three) which occur whilst Jesus is in the Temple precincts (chapters 21-22). Matthew is very close to Mark in this incident.
4. Harrington, p.299; Byrne, p.161. Wright, 2:75, observes that the central issue is really whether Jesus thought he was the Messiah, since the Messiah would have authority over the Temple.
5. 11:9; 14:1-12; 17:11-13. Jesus shares this view (11:9).
6. 26:3,47
7. Davies & Allison, p.358.
8. There are three different manuscript versions of the parable. For details see Green, p.178; Harrington, p.299; Senior, p.237; Meier, *Matthew*, p.240; Beare, p.424. Most scholars concur with the NRSV.
9. Senior, p.237, notes that mention of the vineyard links this parable with the one which follows.
10. Davies & Allison, p.360. They note that Jesus' opponents are adept at laying traps but not at avoiding falling into them themselves. Jesus is much cleverer on both scores.
11. Meier, *Matthew*, p.240; see 7:21-23; 12:50; 23:3-4.
12. Isa 5:1-7. Hagner, p.613; Senior, p.237; Meier, *Matthew*, p.241, who suggests also the Kingdom. Davies & Allison, p.359, note the allegorical interpretation: the father represents God, the first son the *sinners*, the second son the chief priests and elders.

13. Meier, *Matthew*, p.241, following Chrysostom, suggests a further meaning: those saying 'yes' could be the Jews; those saying 'no' but changing, the Gentiles. Davies & Allison, p.361, claim that modern exegetes prefer to think of believing and unbelieving Israel.

14. Meier, *Matthew*, p.241; the 2 following parables have this thrust.

15. 7:21

16. 7:24

17. 12:50

18. Byrne, p.161.

19. 6:17-49.The section in Matthew is 11:2-19. Scholars believe that 'Q' is the source for both.

20. 7:1-10 see Advent week 1; 7:11-17. See Winstanley, *Jesus and the Little People*, p.115-118.

21. John's being in prison is not mentioned here as it is in the Matthaean parallel; Luke has mentioned it in 3:20. Green, p.294, notes the close link with what has just been narrated.

22. 3:7-17; in 3:16 the Baptist speaks of the one *more powerful than I* who is coming.

23. 4: 16-21. Green, p.295, notes that 'John's interest lies on the fault line between his eschatological expectations and the realities of Jesus' performance'.

24. The presence of disciples who are aloof from the movement of Jesus is an indication that the Baptist is not convinced of Jesus' role. (Caird, p.111)

25. Isa 61:1; 35:5-6; 26:19; 29:18-19; 42:18; 43:8. Green, p.297, observes that the *overlap with Jesus' inaugural sermon and his answer to John provides a powerful sanction for the integrity of his mission: he is doing what the Spirit of the Lord anointed him to do.* Marshall, p.291, notes that the list refers to the ministry of Jesus as a whole, and is couched in the language of the OT.

26. Byrne, p.71. Caird, p.112; McBride, p.98, calls this *a delicate plea for understanding.*

27. Marshall, p.287, observes that the person who recognises the fulfilment will know that Jesus is the coming One, and will not be put off by his failure to live up to the traditional – or Johannine – expectations.

28. Caird, p.111.

29. The Greek could also be rendered: Why did you go...? See Evans, p.353.

30. Marshall, p.292.

31. Mal 3:1 and also Exod 23:20; John is the end-time prophet proclaimed in scripture. The 'you' now refers to Jesus. The quotation is also found in Mark 1:2.

32. Caird, p.111, points out that Jesus' public testimony to the prophetic greatness of the Baptist entailed the risk of reprisals from Herod.

33. Green, p.299.

34. Byrne, p.72. Caird, p.112: John belonged to the old order – the greatest man who ever lived before the coming of the Kingdom.

35. McBride, p.99; Marshall, p.297; LaVerdiere, p.106, take these verses as an introduction to what follows. Johnson, p.125, holds that the words are Luke's authorial commentary rather than a report of Jesus' words. He also notes that the division in the people evinced here was predicted by Simeon.

36. For the Fourth Gospel see: C.K. Barrett, The Gospel according to John (London, SPCK 1978); T.L. Brodie, The Gospel according to John (Oxford, OUP 1993); R.E. Brown, The Gospel according to John 2 vols (London, Chapmans 1972); W.Carter, John (Peabody, Hendrickson 2006); R.M.Chennattu, Johannine Discipleship as a Covenant Relationship (Peabody, Hendrickson 2006); M.L. Coloe, God Dwells With Us (Collegeville, Liturgical Press 2001); Dwelling in the Household of God (Collegeville, LiturgicalPress 2007); I. de la Potterie, The Hour of Jesus (Slough, St Paul Publications 1989); C.H. Dodd, The Interpretation of the Fourth Gospel (Cambridge, CUP 1968); C.R. Koester, Symbolism in the Fourth Gospel (Minneapolis, Fortress 2003); The Word of Life (Grand Rapids, Eerdmans 2008); R. Kysar, John's Story of Jesus (Philadelphia, Fortress 1984); The Maverick Gospel (Louisville, John Knox Press 2007); D.A. Lee, The Symbolic Narratives of the Fourth Gospel (Sheffield, JSOT 1994); Flesh and Glory (New York,

Crossroad 2002); R.H. Lightfoot, St John's Gospel (Oxford, OUP 1956); A.T. Lincoln, The Gospel according to Saint John, (London, Baker Academic 2013); B. Lindars, The Gospel of John (London, Oliphants 1972); F.J. Moloney, The Gospel of John (Collegeville, Liturgical Press 1998); The Gospel of John, Text and Context (Boston, Brill 2005); Love in the Gospel of John (Grand Rapids, Baker Academic 2013); R. Schnackenburg, The Gospel of John (London, B&O vol.1 1968, vol.2 1980, vol.3 1982); S.M. Schneiders, Written That You May Believe (New York, Crossroad 1999); M.W.G. Stibbe, John. Readings (Sheffield, JSOT Press 1993).
37. John 1:6-9.
38. 4:34
39. Moloney, Love, p.48-50, notes the difference between works and signs. Whilst they can overlap, the negativity which at times is attached to signs (2:23-25; 6:14-15) is never applied to works. After Jesus' death, his disciples will continue his works (14:12). Jesus brings to completion the work given him by the Father through accomplishing in his ministry the works that show his authority as the one sent by God.

The Final Eight Days

Jesus' Family Tree

O ver the last few years a number of my friends became interested in tracing their family trees. I was amazed at their fascination with the project, and with their enthusiasm and commitment. Personally, I have never for a moment felt the slightest temptation to follow their lead. This kind of interest or preoccupation is not, however, simply another modern phenomenon or fad. There are several examples of family trees in the Hebrew Bible, for it was a characteristic feature of that culture. Particularly important for royal, noble or priestly families for the authentication of their claims, it was also necessary for ordinary folk in order to prove that they belonged to a particular tribe. For them it was a passport to survival.[1] So perhaps we shouldn't be surprised that Matthew begins his story of Jesus with a family tree, or a genealogy, as it is technically called. It is important not to be put off by what seems a lengthy list of unpronounceable names, for there is great richness in these verses.

In this, of course, Matthew differs from Mark who begins his Gospel with the adult Jesus coming to John for baptism by the Jordan River. Even earlier, Paul, writing in about AD 50, whilst mentioning that Jesus was, *born of a woman, born a subject of the Law*,[2] does not suggest anything exceptional or unusual about Jesus' birth, and shows no interest in exploring it. It is Matthew and Luke, who, probably writing in the mid or late AD 80, choose to launch their Gospel story with what is usually referred to as *an Infancy Narrative*.[3] The Gospel readings for the rest of Advent are all taken from these two very different narratives.

It is Matthew's genealogy which provides the Gospel reading for today.

An account of the genealogy of Jesus the Messiah, the son of David, the son of Abraham. Abraham was the father of Isaac, and Isaac the father of Jacob, and Jacob the father of Judah and his brothers, and Judah the father of Perez and Zerah by Tamar, and Perez the father of Hezron, and Hezron the father of Aram, and Aram the father of Aminadab, and Aminadab the father of Nahshon, and Nahshon the father of Salmon, and Salmon the father of Boaz by Rahab, and Boaz the father of Obed by Ruth, and Obed the father of Jesse, and Jesse the father of King David.

And David was the father of Solomon by the wife of Uriah, and Solomon the father of Rehoboam, and Rehoboam the father of Abijah, and Abijah the father of Asaph, and Asaph the father of Jehoshaphat, and Jehoshaphat the father of Joram, and Joram the father of Uzziah, and Uzziah the father of Jotham, and Jotham the father of Ahaz, and Ahaz the father of Hezekiah, and Hezekiah the father of Manasseh, and Manasseh the father of Amos, and Amos the father of Josiah, and Josiah the father of Jechoniah and his brothers, at the time of the deportation to Babylon.

And after the deportation to Babylon: Jechoniah was the father of Salathiel, and Salathiel the father of Zerubbabel, and Zerubbabel the father of Abiud, and Abiud the father of Eliakim, and Eliakim the father of Azor, and Azor the father of Zadok, and Zadok the father of Achim, and Achim the father of Eliud, and Eliud the father of Eleazar, and Eleazar the father of Matthan, and Matthan the father of Jacob, and Jacob the father of Joseph the husband of Mary, of whom Jesus was born, who is called the Messiah.

So all the generations from Abraham to David are fourteen generations; and from David to the deportation to Babylon, fourteen generations; and from the deportation to Babylon to the Messiah, fourteen generations. (Matt 1:1-17)

Matthew's opening statement is more than a simple introduction. Here, right at the outset of his Gospel, the evangelist is laying out his stall, revealing his own faith stance, making evident the perspective from which he is writing. For him, Jesus, whose story he is embarking upon, is *the Christ* (the Messiah or anointed one), the *Son of David*, the *Son of Abraham*. Jesus is proclaimed as the one who has brought to fulfilment the Jewish messianic hopes, the one who is heir to the promises made long before to King David, and heir to the promises for all the nations made even earlier to the great patriarch Abraham.[4]

The genealogy firmly anchors Jesus in the history of his people; he is one with Israel. It is divided into three major sections. It begins with the patriarchal period, in which God's providence, originality and freedom are evidenced in choices made: Isaac rather than Ishmael, Jacob rather than Esau, Judah amongst the sons of Jacob.[5] It then moves on to the monarchic times. Most kings in the list were not faithful to God's law; they did not fulfil their responsibilities at all well. The dividing points in the genealogy, the reign of David and the exile, indicate that Jesus is one with his people in the highs and lows of their history.[6]

Matthew gives emphasis to the number fourteen. It probably indicates Jesus' connection with David, for in some circles at that time letters of the alphabet were accorded numerical significance. David is 4-6-4, which equals 14. The threefold repetition probably indicates that Jesus is the perfection of the Davidic line. Matthew does have some mathematical problems with his counting, as there are not 14 generations in each of the sections![7] Another slant on this issue is offered by the fact that apocalyptic thought at the time divided the history of the world into neat periods of sevens, consisting in weeks of years. Matthew has three sets of two weeks (six sevens). Jesus thus begins the seventh period, the number of fulfilment and perfection. Whilst we may feel bemused by this, number symbolism was not unusual in the world of Matthew.[8] For Matthew, all this is intended to illustrate

God's marvellous providence, God's guiding hand, in carefully planning the flow of Israel's history, in and through the chaos and the problems, in its movement towards the Messiah.[9] Jesus is the climax of the whole list. His coming is what Israel has been awaiting for some 2000 years. There is a dynamic sense that the time has now come.[10]

The names found in the list of ancestors suggest that Jesus' lineage is not racially pure or without sin.[11] Unlike Luke, Josephus, or Old Testament writers, Matthew mentions four women in his genealogy, which is culturally most unusual. Women of courage and initiative, those named play significant roles in the unfolding of Israel's history and of God's purposes. The four are probably Gentiles; and, like many of the males in the list, may be considered as sinners.[12] In a patriarchal society as Gentiles and as women they were on the margins. Perhaps the main reason for their presence in the genealogy is the fact that there was something irregular in their marital situation, and yet this was not an obstacle to their being caught up in God's saving design. God indeed writes straight with crooked lines. This pattern serves as a preparation for the story of Mary. Matthew's inclusive decision is best explained by the combination of the scandalous or irregular union and of divine intervention through the women.[13] The providence of God in the unfolding of this lengthy list of generations is evident.

The regular rhythm of the genealogy is broken when Matthew does not state that Joseph is the father of Jesus. The pattern is altered in that he is presented as the husband of Mary, of whom Jesus was born, who is called the Messiah. The explanation of this change is provided in the subsequent narrative.

Reflections

Whilst not being an enthusiast for family trees, I believe that this reading invites all of us to recognise with gratitude the people who have contributed to making us who we are, people within our family and people beyond, like educators, doctors, pastors and friends.

We could explore our sense of belonging to a particular group, culture, nation, church, community, and what that means for us.

We are, at least in part, the product of so many factors of history, fashioned to a large extent by our place of origin, our local upbringing, our national heritage, our religion. These factors have influenced our thinking and attitudes, our outlook and prejudices. Not all influences have been positive, admittedly, and we may need to come to terms with this, and seek healing.

I am English, with some Irish ancestry, from Wigan in Lancashire, born an only child into a Catholic, ordinary working-class family, brought up in the country with fields and space all around, with a musical and sporting father and religious mother, and I was educated by the Salesians. I see God's providential care and love present in all this, and that care goes back even for centuries on a very broad canvas. All this and much more is a given; what I do with it is my responsibility and opportunity and challenge. Advent offers me a setting in which I am encouraged to acknowledge all this, to be deeply grateful, and to open myself to God's ongoing enlivening and transforming presence.

In our reflecting we might also be able to trace the providence of God in our lives and history too. We can perhaps isolate one or two people, moments, situations or events which, in humble faith, we might identify as *providential*, as indications that in and through the ups and downs of our experience, our loving, faithful and saving God is around, actively present, and is with us.

Through the genealogy, Matthew presents Jesus as a member of the human family, and especially as at one with the history of his people. He is rooted in Israel. It is worth noting that the mix of saint and sinner found in the genealogy is repeated in the ministry of Jesus, and subsequently in the history of the Church as far as you and me today. There is a healthy realism about this evangelist. God's style has not changed; God continues to work with us in the twists and turn of our lives today. And God is very patient, caring and always faithful. We can entrust ourselves to Him.

December 18th

The Birth and Naming Of Jesus

The Gospel extract chosen for today continues Matthew's Infancy Narrative. The evangelist has clearly proclaimed his faith in Jesus as the Messiah, Son of David and Son of Abraham. He now switches from genealogy to narrative. He explains the reason behind his changing the pattern of the genealogy by not indicating the paternity of Joseph, and clarifies how it comes about that Jesus is Son of David. Furthermore, he proclaims Jesus' identity as Son of God.

Now the birth of Jesus the Messiah took place in this way. When his mother Mary had been engaged to Joseph, but before they lived together, she was found to be with child from the Holy Spirit. Her husband Joseph, being a righteous man and unwilling to expose her to public disgrace, planned to dismiss her quietly. But just when he had resolved to do this, an angel of the Lord appeared to him in a dream and said, *Joseph, son of David, do not be afraid to take Mary as your wife, for the child conceived in her is from the Holy Spirit. She will bear a son, and you are to name him Jesus, for he will save his people from their sins.* All this took place to fulfil what had been spoken by the Lord through the prophet: *Look, the virgin shall conceive and bear a son, and they shall name him Emmanuel,* which means, *God is with us.* When Joseph awoke from sleep, he did as the angel of the Lord commanded him; he took her as his wife, but had no marital relations with her until she had borne a son; and he named him Jesus. (Matt 1:18-25)

Matthew informs us how the birth of Jesus the Messiah took place, again repeating that title. The main characters are introduced, Mary and Joseph, who were betrothed, but had not yet come to live together.[14] Jewish matrimonial procedure entailed two steps. Firstly, betrothal took place, which was a formal exchange of consent in the presence of two witnesses. Usually this occurred when the girl was 12 or 13 years of age. The English term *engaged*, adopted in the above translation, does not accurately describe Jewish practice, because betrothal was considered a legally ratified marriage, and the obligations undertaken were binding. In fact, the man was known as husband immediately, and the woman passed from the authority of her father to that of the husband. Any infringement of marital rights was considered to be adultery. If the man died, the girl was treated as a widow. The second stage took place a year or so later, when the bride went to live with her husband in his home, and the marriage was consummated. Some scholars maintain that at least in Galilee marital intercourse was tolerated for a betrothed couple.

The reader is informed that through the creative action of the Holy Spirit, and without the agency of any male, Mary is with child. Her pregnancy throws Joseph into crisis, for he knows he is not responsible for this.[15] As a devout, law-abiding Jew he feels obliged to divorce her.[16] As a compassionate man, he decides to adopt the less public divorce procedure, which could take place without a formal enquiry, and would protect her from public disgrace. But he has a dream, a revelation from God, which changes all that.

Dreams are a feature of Matthew's Infancy Narrative. The five examples found there follow the same basic stereotyped literary format: the Angel of the Lord appears and gives *a message/ command*, with an accompanying explanation of the rationale behind the action indicated; then Joseph immediately obeys to the letter. The only exception to the template is this first dream, which is more complex because it contains elements of an annunciation of birth narrative; such narratives have their own template or pattern.[17]

Joseph, addressed as Son of David,[18] is told not to be afraid to complete the marriage process by taking Mary home as his wife. The angel then explains that her pregnancy is the result of the action of the Holy Spirit. This is the heart of the message. Following the normal pattern of such annunciations, Joseph is assured that she will in time give birth, and he is told what the child's name is to be, with an etymological explanation of the name, which also describes the child's role or mission from God.[19] The presence of the creative and life-giving power of the Spirit was in the New Testament initially associated with the resurrection of Jesus, then, working backwards, with the baptism of Jesus and the opening of his mission. Now it is related to the very beginning of Jesus' life, not through sexual intervention but through the same power of the Spirit that brought life into the world at the creation.[20] Joseph now knows that Mary has not been unfaithful and that the Law has not been infringed.

The child's name, given by God, is to be Jesus. This was a fairly common name in first century Palestine. It was a derivative of the name Joshua, the successor of Moses, who led the people of Israel into the land of promise. Originally the name meant *Yahweh helps*, but in popular etymology the meaning had come to be understood as *Yahweh saves.* The angel links this meaning with Jesus' name; his role in life will be to save his people. The word *people* is probably to be understood here more widely than simply the people of Israel; it includes both Jews and Gentiles.[21] This salvation, surprisingly for that time in the history of Israel, is not nationalistic liberation from economic or political oppression, which was the common expectation, but from their sins and the consequences of their sin.[22] Saving from sins becomes a way of characterising the whole messianic mission of Jesus.[23]

A scriptural quotation provides further insight into his identity and role.[24] Such quotations, often referred to as *formula quotations,* are a feature of Matthew's Gospel, which contains about twelve of them. Their purpose is to show that the New Testament is the fulfilment of the Old. It was a way of proving that God had foretold Jesus' career, and that everything, even minor details, was part of God's plan.

Matthew uses this technique to considerable effect in the Infancy Narrative, with great art, originality and freedom. The references provide us with insight into his theological message, particularly his Christological emphases.

Here, Matthew applies a passage from Isaiah (7:14) to the virginal situation of Mary's pregnancy; and Jesus is proclaimed to be *Emmanuel*, meaning *God is with us*. The God, who was present with Israel throughout its history, is now present with God's people in a new and very special way. This oracle was originally addressed to King Ahaz in a situation of political and military crisis in 8th century Judah. It concerned the imminent birth of a child to be conceived in the normal way by a young woman, who was probably a royal princess. The child would be a sign of God's saving presence with Ahaz and the people. Some commentators think that the child in question was Hezekiah, who proved to be a truly religious monarch. Matthew creatively adapts the quotation to his own infancy context and his theological purpose.[25] In the previous verse Ahaz is addressed as House of David, so both aspects of Jesus' identity are linked.[26] Later Matthew concludes his Gospel with the Risen Christ promising to be with his disciples always until the end of time.[27]

On awaking, Joseph follows the angel's instructions to the letter. His response to God is always one of complete obedience. He takes Mary to his home as his wife, assuming responsibility for her and for the child she is carrying. In time she gives birth to a son, and Joseph names him Jesus. The emphasis is placed on the naming rather than the birth, which is mentioned only in a passing phrase. In this way Joseph becomes the legal father of Jesus, and Jesus becomes a member of the Davidic line.[28] He is Son of David and also Son of God. His being Son of Abraham will be described in the subsequent chapter, with the coming to Bethlehem of the Gentile Magi.

Reflections

Matthew's presentation of the birth and naming of Jesus is very gentle and sensitive. We catch something of the angst and turmoil of Joseph on discovering that Mary is pregnant. We are left to imagine Mary's confusion and fear too. The God of love, however, is not far away. Joseph in Matthew's story comes across as a man of principle and compassion. This is a wonderful blending of qualities which we can strive to emulate. In this and in subsequent episodes he obeys to the letter the will of God as it is presented to him. This too is a key element of spirituality as the evangelist presents it. It is also a key feature of Jesus' own life and ministry, and an element of his preaching. In the dreams the will of God was clearly outlined for Joseph. Even though we are aware that God's will is always that we do what love demands, there can be occasions when what this entails in a given situation is not too evident. We are called to ponder and discern, and then respond as best we see fit.

In this brief Gospel extract, Jesus is proclaimed by Matthew as our Saviour. He comes to save us from our sins, from whatever hinders our relationship with God. As readers, we are obliged to wait to learn how this will take place as the story unfolds, but we are aware of our ongoing need for salvation, and our hope is immediately aroused. Whenever we mention the name of Jesus, we call on him as saviour. Jesus is also presented as our Emmanuel, a name which assures us that God is with us. This tells us so much about the love of God for us, God's desire to be near to us, to be a constant in our lives. In Jesus, God's presence is expressed in a human being with a name. Perhaps we have grown too accustomed to this extraordinary statement, and yet have not begun to fathom its depth. Advent affords us the opportunity to reflect on and absorb God's saving presence in all the twists and turns of our lives. As we think about this, we may discover that God's presence is often mediated by other people, who can listen and show they care. And this may remind us of our responsibility as disciples of Jesus to try humbly and gently to be instruments of that presence for others.

In this story we encounter Joseph, a dreamer, like his earlier namesake. The rich blending of reverence for the Law of his people and deep human compassion makes him an attractive character. In this, and in subsequent episodes, he is presented as one who listens to what is revealed to him by God in his dreams, and then responds obeying it without delay and to the letter. He is a model of obedience, and probably quite a challenge to each of us. There are dreams and dreams! Often we are faced with situations in which it isn't easy to discern God's will and we'd appreciate a revelatory dream or two! Perhaps what really matters is our desire to be open and to be true to our God in the decisions we make. The words of Jesus as he defends the woman who has anointed him in the house of Simon of Bethany are affirming and encouraging: *She has done what she could.*[29]

December 19th

The Annunciation To Zechariah

After reflecting on the opening chapter of Matthew's Gospel in the last two days, we are now invited for the rest of the build-up to Christmas to ponder the first chapter of Luke.[30]This unfolds in the following sequence: the annunciation of the Baptist's birth; the annunciation of the birth of Jesus; the visit of Mary to Elizabeth; the Magnificat; the birth and naming of the Baptist; the Benedictus. As was noted with Matthew's Infancy Narrative, themes and issues which are central to the whole Gospel find their first airing here, overture-like.

Omitting Luke's brief introduction to the Gospel, the storyline commences:

In the days of King Herod of Judea, there was a priest named Zechariah, who belonged to the priestly order of Abijah. His wife was a descendant of Aaron, and her name was Elizabeth. Both of them were righteous before God, living blamelessly according to all the commandments and regulations of the Lord. But they had no children, because Elizabeth was barren, and both were getting on in years.

Once when he was serving as priest before God and his section was on duty, he was chosen by lot, according to the custom of the priesthood, to enter the sanctuary of the Lord and offer incense. Now at the time of the incense-offering, the whole assembly of the people was praying outside. Then there appeared to him an angel of the Lord, standing at the right side of the altar of incense. When Zechariah saw him, he was terrified; and fear overwhelmed him. But the angel said to him, *Do not be afraid, Zechariah, for your prayer has been heard. Your wife Elizabeth will bear you a son, and you will name him 'John'.*

113

You will have joy and gladness, and many will rejoice at his birth, for he will be great in the sight of the Lord. He must never drink wine or strong drink; even before his birth he will be filled with the Holy Spirit. He will turn many of the people of Israel to the Lord their God. With the spirit and power of Elijah he will go before him, to turn the hearts of parents to their children, and the disobedient to the wisdom of the righteous, to make ready a people prepared for the Lord. Zechariah said to the angel, *How will I know that this is so? For I am an old man, and my wife is getting on in years.* The angel replied, *I am Gabriel. I stand in the presence of God, and I have been sent to speak to you and to bring you this good news. But now, because you did not believe my words, which will be fulfilled in their time, you will become mute, unable to speak, until the day these things occur.*

Meanwhile, the people were waiting for Zechariah, and wondered at his delay in the sanctuary. When he did come out, he could not speak to them, and they realized that he had seen a vision in the sanctuary. He kept motioning to them and remained unable to speak. When his time of service was ended, he went to his home.

After those days his wife Elizabeth conceived, and for five months she remained in seclusion. She said, *This is what the Lord has done for me when he looked favourably on me and took away the disgrace I have endured among my people.*

(Luke 1:5-25)

Luke begins his narrative by setting the scene, describing the context and introducing the characters.[31] The events which he is to recount take place in Judea during the reign of King Herod the Great, a Roman appointee who ruled Palestine.[32]

The territory which he governed stretched more widely than Judea itself, it included Samaria and Galilee.[33] The leading human characters in the story are brought on stage, Zechariah and his wife,

114

Elizabeth. Zechariah, whose name means *Yahweh remembers*, is a priest. Elizabeth too, as a descendant of Aaron, comes from a priestly family.[34] They are presented as an upright and deeply religious couple, obediently observing the Law with meticulous care. God is clearly at the centre of their lives.[35] However, they have to bear the sorrow of having no children, which were popularly thought to be a sign of God's blessing, their absence a token of God's displeasure.[36] Elizabeth is said to be barren, which was a stigma, a painfully felt reproach for a Jewish woman. Given that the couple are elderly, their situation is, humanly speaking, beyond hope.

The situation of Elizabeth and Zechariah contains echoes of situations found in a number of Old Testament narratives. There we come across several stories of barren women who become capable of bearing children as a result of God's intervention: Sarah, Rebecca, Rachel, the unnamed mother of Samson, and Hannah. In the case of Abraham and Sarah, both were also very old. Luke's narrative recalls in a particular way the stories of Abraham and Sarah, and Elkanah and Hannah, the parents of Isaac and Samuel respectively.[37] Perhaps God will perform the impossible again.

The story moves forward with the information that Zechariah is on duty fulfilling his priestly responsibilities in the Jerusalem Temple. The Gospel itself, as well as the Infancy Narrative, opens and closes in this Temple setting.[38] This is a clear link with Israel's past. All the male descendants of Aaron were priests, entitled to officiate at Temple worship. Each group served in rotation for a week every six months. Given such numbers, the morning and evening duties were assigned by lot.[39] This leaves space for the intervention of God; God is at work in the choice. The high point of a priest's life was to enter the sanctuary or Holy Place, situated next to the Holy of Holies, at the time of sacrifice and burn incense on the altar which stood in its centre.[40] After this, he would come outside and bless the people, who are engaged in prayer. This was a once in a lifetime experience, since a priest could not perform the task again until all the others of his division had done so.

Consequently, this would be the greatest day in Zechariah's life. As he carries out this coveted task, probably in the early evening, the people in considerable numbers, a frequent Lucan feature, remain outside in prayer to their God.

It is in the setting of this Holy Place that the Good News of the inauguration of God's saving plan is announced.[41] For, suddenly *an angel of the Lord* appears to Zechariah on the right side, the place of honour and favour. God is actively present in His sanctuary through this heavenly messenger. *The angel of the Lord* is a figure commonly found in scriptural stories of this kind. Originally, the angel was not thought of as a personal being, but was simply a reverential way of describing God's presence. After the exile and contact with Persia, an angelology developed in which angels were conceived of as personal intermediaries.[42] Not unnaturally, Zechariah is disturbed by this visionary experience, and fearful. The angel seeks to allay his fear by assuring him that his prayer has been heard by God, a motif which occurs frequently in this Gospel. Zechariah's formal prayer, in unison with the people outside, would have been for the salvation of Israel; but he was probably also praying for the gift of a son. Both story lines are brought together through God's intervention, as individual and national longings are set to be fulfilled.[43]

God's angel proceeds to announce to him the Good News that his wife will bear a son, and that he must be given the name John. This was not an uncommon name; it was popularly taken to mean God has been gracious, though this etymology is not explicitly supplied. His name is thus imposed by God, and indicates something about his role in God's design. The boy will be a source of joy and delight for them, and his birth will be the occasion of widespread rejoicing beyond the family circle, for it has implications for the salvation of all the people.

The angel then speaks at some length in rhythmic, poetic style about this child's future role and significance. *He will be great in the sight of God, set apart and utterly dedicated to God's service, abstaining from wine and strong drink as did the Nazirites of old,*[44] without being one himself in the full sense of the term. Even before birth he will be filled with the Holy Spirit, a clear indication of God's special choice,[45] and thus empowered he will carry out a prophetic role, the mission of conversion, bringing a repentant people of Israel back to their God. His role will be evocative of the great reformer prophet Elijah, as he prepares a people for the coming of God,[46] turning the hearts of fathers to the children,[47] and turning the disobedient to the wisdom of the upright.[48] He will thus take his place in a succession of prophetic figures through whom God visits his people.[49]

Zechariah then asks, not how this is to occur, given the factor of the couple's age, but how he is to know it, how he can be sure. In his unbelief, he seeks a proof, a frequent Jewish failing, which is a way of usurping the initiative which belongs to God.[50] In reply the angel now discloses his identity and credentials: he is Gabriel, who stands in God's presence as a special servant, and who has been sent by God to deliver this gladdening news. Since his message comes from God, it is utterly reliable and will inevitably come true; the prophecy will be duly fulfilled.[51] The giving of a sign is part of the literary form. Here Gabriel decrees that Zechariah will be struck dumb until the event occurs. This sign can be interpreted in different ways. It could be a punishment for unbelief, a means of preserving the content and wonder of the revelation from the people at large until later, a warning that something new is breaking in, which demands great faith.[52] In fact, Zechariah is himself the sign for others that something quite mysterious has taken place in the Temple.[53]

The scene now changes, reverting to the wider Temple area. The people outside have become aware of the delay, and they are surprised. When the priest eventually emerges from the sanctuary to give the customary blessing, he is unable to speak. The people realise that he has had a vision. After concluding his term of office, Zechariah returns home to the country. Sometime later his wife becomes pregnant.

She gratefully recognises that this is the result of God's gracious kindness, a kindness which has also removed her public humiliation.[54] She withdraws from social life, remaining in the seclusion of her home. The reason for this is not evident. Some suggest that it is an indication of awe before the workings of God; others it is to avoid further reproach until the pregnancy is evident, or to remain in prayer. Most probably, it is a literary device to prepare for the revelation of the unknown pregnancy to Mary, who becomes the first to know.[55] Five months would be half the pregnancy according to the more common reckoning of ten lunar months.

Already in this opening section of the Infancy Narrative we have met some of the themes which will recur throughout Luke's Gospel: Jerusalem and the Temple; the grouping of the whole people; the importance and efficacy of prayer; God's reversing human expectations and perceptions; the importance of women; the presence of the Spirit; joy; prophecy and fulfilment. But above all, it is clear that God is the central actor. Everything stems from God's free, faithful and compassionate love.

Reflections

Poverty can assume many forms. Today's reading and the stories which constitute its scriptural background highlight the poverty of childlessness. In the culture of the near east it was a source of shame for a woman not to bear children. We sense the disappointment and hopelessness of the elderly couple Elizabeth and Zechariah. The God of surprises intervenes dramatically, announcing the reversal of this situation, the lifting of this heavy burden. The couple's prayer will be answered, Elizabeth will have a child, who will be their *joy and delight*. And this child will have a significant role in the unfolding of God's saving plan, *preparing for the Lord a people fit for him*. He is the answer to the elderly couple's prayers and the communal prayers of centuries.

We all experience our own forms of poverty; we have burdens to carry, dreams unfulfilled, longings unanswered, perhaps a sense of failure and hopelessness. This is not an indication of God's displeasure. It is an unavoidable aspect of human living. Our reading invites us to trust in the God of surprises, who seems to delight in turning things upside down. It assures us that God will listen to our prayers, but will do so in God's own way and time. Situations can be changed beyond our wildest dreams and imagining. From other situations, even if they remain unchanged, lasting and unexpected good can be drawn.

The God behind Luke's story is above all a God of joy, a God who remembers us graciously and with favour, and whose love is generous and overflowing. In Advent we are invited to allow this God to touch our lives. Today's episode ends on a wonderfully symbolic and perhaps comical note: a pregnant old lady and a dumb old man, who have become the makers of history.[56]

The Annunciation To Mary

The annunciation of the angel Gabriel to Zechariah is followed immediately and in parallel by the annunciation to Mary, a scriptural passage with which we are all very familiar, a scene famously and imaginatively depicted in art and music. The narrative follows very closely the basic literary pattern for biblical annunciations of birth.

In the sixth month the angel Gabriel was sent by God to a town in Galilee called Nazareth, to a virgin engaged to a man whose name was Joseph, of the house of David. The virgin's name was Mary. And he came to her and said, *Greetings, favoured one! The Lord is with you.* But she was much perplexed by his words and pondered what sort of greeting this might be. The angel said to her, *Do not be afraid, Mary, for you have found favour with God. And now, you will conceive in your womb and bear a son, and you will name him Jesus. He will be great, and will be called the Son of the Most High, and the Lord God will give to him the throne of his ancestor David. He will reign over the house of Jacob for ever, and of his kingdom there will be no end.* Mary said to the angel, *How can this be, since I am a virgin?* The angel said to her, *The Holy Spirit will come upon you, and the power of the Most High will overshadow you; therefore the child to be born will be holy; he will be called Son of God. And now, your relative Elizabeth in her old age has also conceived a son; and this is the sixth month for her who was said to be barren. For nothing will be impossible with God.* Then Mary said, *Here am I, the servant of the Lord; let it be with me according to your word.* Then the angel departed from her. (Luke 1:26-38)

Luke introduces the second episode of his Infancy Narrative with an indication of time, the sixth month, which links the story with the preceding incident, Elizabeth's miraculous pregnancy which is not known yet by any outsider because of her five month confinement. The location has switched northwards from the city of Jerusalem and its Temple and priestly setting, to provincial Galilee and an insignificant little hamlet, which Luke typically calls a city (polis) named *Nazareth*. The two characters of the story are then brought on stage: the angel Gabriel once more (which means that God is the major protagonist) and a young virgin named Mary.[57] She is said to be betrothed to Joseph, a member of the house of David; the text probably does not imply that Mary too is of David's line.[58] The Jewish marriage process, as we have seen, consisted in two stages: there was a betrothal ceremony in which consent was exchanged in the presence of witnesses, and then, after an interval of about a year, the two came to live together. This betrothal ceremony was a legally binding contract, so that technically Mary was Joseph's wife, though the couple had not yet begun to live together.[59]

The contrast between Zechariah and Mary is quite breathtaking. He is a priest functioning in the Temple at the pulsating centre of national life. Mary holds no official position among the people. Whereas he is described as righteous and law-abiding, she is among the most powerless people in her society: she is young in a world that values age; female in a world ruled by men; poor in a stratified economy. Luke understands God's activity as surprising and often paradoxical, almost always reversing human expectations.[60]

The narrative proceeds according to the normal structural pattern of annunciation stories, and the parallels with the description of Gabriel's visiting of Zechariah are strikingly close. The two accounts are frequently referred to as a diptych.[61] The angel appears to Mary indoors, in the midst of her everyday life, and greets her with great respect. *Chaire* (*Hail*) is a customary formal manner of address; it can also mean *rejoice*.[62] He calls her *favoured one*, or *You who enjoys God's favour*. The two words have closely related stems in Greek, and alliteration is employed.

In all that is happening, the initiative rests with God, with God's unconditional choice. She is assured that God is with her, an expression found frequently in the Old Testament;[63] it conveys the guarantee of God's help, support and empowerment for the one chosen to serve Him.

Mary is deeply disturbed by what she hears, utterly confused, terrified even, and wonders about its meaning and implications.[64] The angel calms her fears, telling her not to be afraid, an injunction typical of annunciation stories. In words which have a poetic ring, he again assures her of God's gracious choice and initiative, and spells out his message. She is to conceive and bear a son. She is to call the child Jesus, which was quite a common name at the time, and means *Yahweh saves*, though, perhaps surprisingly, such etymology is not given. It was normally the father who named the child, but there are precedents for women doing so;[65] we are later informed that they gave him the name Jesus.

The identity and role of the child are then spelled out. He will be great, a greatness measured by his title *Son of the Most High*.[66] By God's gift he will accede to the Davidic throne as the royal Messiah, and will rule forever. The phrasing of these verses echoes Nathan's promise to David, but the idea of a line of descendants ruling forever is changed to the idea that the Messiah himself will reign everlastingly.[67] The House of Jacob is an archaic synonym for Israel.[68] These are conventional Jewish messianic hopes and expectations.[69]

Following the usual pattern, Mary seeks information as to how such a conception is to take place, given that she has not a sexual relationship with Joseph or any man. Her question is different from that of Zechariah, who sought a way of knowing God's action. She is not doubting like him and sceptically demanding a proof. Her question highlights the action of God in all this, and affords the opportunity for the angel to further clarify the true origin, identity and manner of conception of the child in a response which far exceeds the religious and cultural expectations of Israel.[70]

The two phrases, *The Holy Spirit will come upon you,* and *The power of the Most High will overshadow you;* are in poetic parallel, and lead into the third phrase: *Therefore the child to be born will be holy; he will be called Son of God.* What is to happen is the result of God's activity and power. *Come upon* is used of the Spirit also in Luke's description of Pentecost.[71] *Overshadow* recalls the creation scene, the spirit's brooding presence over the waters. It is also used of God's glory and presence resting on the tabernacle and protecting God's people, and is used later in the Gospel in the transfiguration scene.[72] Thus the imagery and language, which in the baptism and transfiguration scenes of the Gospel are connected with Jesus being proclaimed as God's Son, are combined here in the annunciation. Jesus' being holy and Son of God is linked with the action of the Spirit. *Something new is breaking in, surpassing anything that has happened before.*[73] Luke's main idea seems to be that of creativity, total newness. Mary is not longing for a child like Zechariah and Elizabeth are; nor is there a prayerful request. Just as the Spirit's action brought life to earth's void, so the Spirit's action brings life to the void of Mary's womb. What is happening is entirely God's surprise, the result of God's initiative.

Mary, without having asked for a sign, is given information which functions as a sign, and this will confirm the trustworthiness of the angel's proclamation. Something deemed impossible has occurred in the life of her kinswoman Elizabeth, now six months pregnant in her old age. This illustrates that for God nothing is impossible. The phrasing echoes God's question to Abraham after Sarah's laughter: *Can anything said by God be impossible?*[74] This is the first hint of any family link between the two women; their stories and the stories of their children are interwoven.[75]

Mary then accepts the role graciously offered to her in the unfolding of God's plan; she receives God into her life in a new way. Open and humble, she expresses her willingness to obey and be of service unreservedly, cost what it may.[76]

> You see before you the Lord's servant,
> let it happen to me as you have said.

Mary joins the line of women who have served God's purposes throughout Israel's history. The language of Mary's reply is not that of the usual literary pattern. Her response heralds the Lucan theme of discipleship. For later in the gospel, in Luke's thorough adaptation of the Markan episode in which Jesus speaks about his true family, we read:

His mother and his brothers came looking for him, but they could not get to him because of the crowd. He was told, *Your mother and brothers are standing outside and want to see you.* But he said in answer, *My mother and my brothers are those who hear the word of God and put it into practice.* (8:19-21)

Mary fulfils the criteria for family membership, for discipleship. In receiving the message of God in the annunciation and in her generous response, she shows that she is a woman of faith, as Elizabeth will shortly recognise. She is, in fact, the first disciple; her discipleship will continue during the ministry of her son, and onwards after the resurrection.[77] After her accepting response, the angel departs. The scenes of Luke's Infancy Narrative generally terminate with departures. *Mary becomes the literal embodiment of the promise of God.*[78]

Reflections

Some of the statements made by Gabriel to Mary in the Gospel extract, which we have been considering, can, I believe, be applied with a different nuance to us and to our situation today.

Do not be afraid, Mary is told. I'm not a mathematician, but I suspect that this must rank as the most reiterated command or commandment in the Bible. These words are addressed so frequently to individuals or groups or the whole people in all kinds of critical situations in Israel's history. I think that fear is at the core of the power of darkness; perhaps it is the original sin. Fear holds us back from surrendering to God. Perhaps it is the fear of losing ourselves, being taken over, losing control over our lives; maybe it is the fear of being found wanting, being inadequate.

Fear makes trust extremely difficult. Fear often prevents us from reaching out to others; it is an obstacle to friendship and intimacy, to community and collaboration, to service and self-giving.

Fear can stifle compassion. Fear thwarts growth, deadens dreams, cramps initiative, crushes potential and saps life's energy. Fear can hinder genuine discernment. So much of the violence and aggression within us and around us in our country and our wider world is born of fear, and is sustained and fuelled by it. We can be afraid of people being different or holding different views. We can be afraid of failure, of what others may think or say. We can be afraid of challenge, of losing control, of being marginalised, of becoming useless. We can be afraid of suffering and of death. Perhaps this Advent we can mull over the fears currently within us, and explore how fear finds expression in our lives now. As we get in touch with our fears, let us hear the word of God brought by the angel: *Do not be afraid.*[79]

The reason why we need not fear is made clear: *the Lord is with you.* In so many of the scriptural narratives where a call is involved and a person is given a special role to fulfil in the unfolding of God's plan, God offers this kind of reassurance. In Mary's situation God is present with her in a truly unique manner. But these reassuring words are addressed to us too. At every stage in our journey, in every situation in which we find ourselves, in all our ups and downs and twists and turns, the Lord is with us. We are always in the heart of God; God's love surrounds us. Maybe the problem here is not God being with us, but our being aware of God's presence, our trusting that this is in fact the case. Awareness can grow as a result of frequent reflection on what is going on in our daily life; it often comes with hindsight. It can grow through silent, wordless prayer. Such awareness strengthens our trust for the future. But at the end of the day the only way to learn how to trust is to trust. We have to take God at his word and surrender. There is no alternative.

Mary is the favoured one, the chosen one amongst all women, as Elizabeth will proclaim later, chosen to be the mother of the one who will be called the Son of God. But we too are blessed, favoured. Each one of us is uniquely chosen, is singled out, as Mark would put it, to be a disciple of Jesus, and to live out that discipleship in a personal way.[80] There is no mass production, no automated assembly line here, no cloning. One of life's mysteries is always, *Why me?* The answer is doubtless that which is found throughout the scriptures: the free and gratuitous love of God. That love is behind Mary's choice and behind the whole story of Jesus. And our *being a chosen one* is an ongoing experience. The message of both the Old and New Testaments is that God is faithful to the choice made; the choice is not withdrawn. God's love cannot change. Each one of us remains chosen, blessed. Perhaps we can pause this Advent to recapture this aspect of who we are.

Mary is chosen to bear a son, to bring Jesus into the world, to give Jesus to the world. This is her role in life, her wonderful mission so crucial to the world's salvation and hope. And it's the birthing of her son that we look forward to with eager anticipation in Advent, reliving that earth-shattering moment liturgically once again. In a different way we too are called and missioned to be bearers of her son to others. For all our fragility and weakness and stumbling, we are sacraments, signs and instruments of the presence of Jesus in our world. Jesus abides within us; he is always with us. We are called to reflect to others something of his compassionate love, his acceptance and care, beginning with those nearest to us. We are invited by the Lord to be *Good News*, to be bearers of healing and hope. It is an awesome responsibility. That's why God tells us not to fear and assures us that he is with us. If we are to mirror the true face of Jesus to one another, and to all those whom we meet, then we need to come to know and love him ever more; and we, like Mary, need the creative and enlivening Spirit to work constantly within us, fashioning and transforming us.

So much for the angel's greeting and message. What about Mary's responses? Gabriel's visit to Nazareth shatters the simplicity and ordinariness of her existence. God's saving plan, God's *Yes* to humankind, is unveiled before her, and she is invited to play a major part in its fulfilment.

Initially her reaction is one of perplexity, which she later articulates in a question, *How can this be?* It's such a lot for her to take in, this approach of her God, this role which she is being invited to accept. Her final response is a quiet *Yes*, uttered with the whole of her being, and resonating till the end of time.

Perhaps the most powerful word in our language is *Yes*. It has the potential to transform faces, situations, lives. It can communicate a response of acceptance, a willingness to share, to collaborate, to become involved. It can convey an openness to change, to welcome what is new, to risk, to move on. It can carry undertones of fear controlled, of hope entertained, of excitement aroused. It can indicate generosity, self-giving, the fullness of love. *Yes* is a word which crosses the lips of a small child, a young woman, an old man. It can be expressed in gesture as well as word. At times it is the empathetic response to mystery, an embracing of the challenge of being alive. We are invited to make Mary's response a paradigm for our daily lives: *You see before you the Lord's servant; let it happen to me as you have said.*

The Visitation

The next scene in Luke's Infancy Narrative brings together the two women who have featured in the annunciation diptych; their two parallel stories are now intertwined within the single story of God's redemption.[81] This episode consists of two parts, both very familiar to us: the visit of Mary to Elizabeth, and then her Magnificat canticle, and her departure. The Advent liturgy separates them for our reflection. The narrative for today, the visitation as we call it, reads as follows:

> In those days Mary set out and went with haste to a Judean town in the hill country, where she entered the house of Zechariah and greeted Elizabeth. When Elizabeth heard Mary's greeting, the child leapt in her womb. And Elizabeth was filled with the Holy Spirit and exclaimed with a loud cry, *Blessed are you among women, and blessed is the fruit of your womb. And why has this happened to me, that the mother of my Lord comes to me? For as soon as I heard the sound of your greeting, the child in my womb leapt for joy. And blessed is she who believed that there would be a fulfilment of what was spoken to her by the Lord.* (Luke 1:39-45)

The action is simply told. After God's saving plan has been revealed to her by the angel, Mary departs from Nazareth in great haste, a promptness which reflects her obedience to God's word.[82] She heads for an unspecified town in the hills of Judah, a seventy to eighty mile journey of about 3-4 days.[83] Many of the priests who served in the Temple lived away from Jerusalem. The parents of Samuel also lived in the hill country.[84] Luke's phrasing, *set out and went*, has a Semitic ring, and recalls the departures of Lot and Abraham.[85] Mary arrives at Zechariah's house, and greets Elizabeth, the older woman, thus bringing her seclusion to an end. The heart of the episode consists in the ensuing dialogue.[86]

The effect on Elizabeth of Mary's greeting is twofold. Firstly, *the child leapt in her womb*. There is perhaps here an allusion to the jostling of Rebecca's twins which heralded their future destinies.[87] This is also an anticipation of the destiny of John, his being gifted with the Spirit from the womb as promised, enabling him to bear prophetic witness to the Coming One whom Mary is carrying. It is a leap of gladness which captures something of the eschatological joy foretold in Gabriel's announcement of his birth. McBride speaks of womb-shaking rejoicing, appropriate for the beginning of the messianic era, the onset of the messianic age of salvation.[88] The second effect is that Elizabeth *was filled with the Holy Spirit*, through whom she comes to realise what God has done for Mary.

Elizabeth is inspired to break into expressions of unrestrained joy and praise, and she proclaims in the form of a short poetic canticle the deep insight revealed to her about God's action in Mary, which far surpasses what God has done for her. Mary, she acknowledges in a kind of prophetic blessing, is blessed by God amongst women, and the child she is carrying within her is also proclaimed to be blessed.[89] In fact, it is precisely because of the child that the mother is so blessed. These words of blessing echo words spoken concerning Judith and Jael, heroines through whom God intervened to save Israel from enemies.[90] Recognising the superior position of her youthful relative, she readily acknowledges that she cannot possibly be worthy of a visit from *the mother of my Lord; Kyrios* is used frequently of God in the Old Testament. In the New Testament, the designation is properly used as a title of the Risen One. Luke frequently uses it of Jesus during the ministry both as a greeting and a title; this is the first instance of such usage, as Elizabeth recognises the child of Mary as Lord and Messiah. There may be an echo of David's words, *How can the Ark come to me?*[91] and the words of Araunah addressed to David standing by the threshing floor, *What is this that my lord the king has come to his servant?*[92]

Elizabeth informs Mary of the movement of her own child within her at her greeting, which the narrator has already informed the reader about.

She concludes her canticle as she began it with words of blessing:

> Blessed is she who believed that the promise made
> her by the Lord would be fulfilled.

The opening word here is *makarios*, the word common in the beatitudes, which is used to recognise a state of being resulting from God's graciousness. Later, during the ministry of Jesus, a woman from the crowd will pronounce blessed the womb and breasts of his mother. To this Jesus replies:

> More blessed still are those who hear the word of
> God and keep it. (11:28)

Elizabeth's blessing is Luke's adaptation of these words. Mary has heard God's word, and has believed that God could and would accomplish what was promised. She perceptively recognises the quality of Mary's listening and belief, a faith and obedience which contrasts with that of her own husband. For Luke, Mary is a model of faith, and already a disciple.[93] Mary responds by breaking into a hymn of praise herself, and this, along with reference to her departure, is the topic for tomorrow's reading.

Reflections

After her momentous meeting with Gabriel, her generous *Yes*, which changed the world forever, Mary doesn't hang around in wonder and amazement, but hastily sets off to make the journey into the Judean hill country, a difficult trek over rough terrain. In self-forgetfulness she desires to be of service to her elderly cousin, to assist her in the normal tasks of everyday around the house, cleaning, washing, fetching water, and just being there. She shares with her the ordinariness of existence, which isn't ordinary any more. To her journeying and her serving she brings the child within her. There is a new dimension to every aspect of her being. When the two expectant mothers meet, Elizabeth recognises God's presence in what is happening to Mary, just as earlier she acknowledged God's compassionate faithfulness in her own life's adventure, and she expresses her wonder.

This moment of encounter is more than simply a meeting of two pregnant mothers: one youthful, one worn and elderly. It is a deeply contemplative moment. This meeting, brimming over with promise and hope and future, is an encounter which occurs within the circle of God's faithful love, God's tender mercy. Both women are in touch with mystery, the transformative presence of God.

All of us, as we go about our ordinary journeys and the humdrum tasks of every day, as we meet people in a wide variety of situations, are invited to perceive the extraordinary dimension of it all. For Jesus is always present in the core of our being, closer to us than we are to ourselves, even though we may fail to notice. And his presence makes a difference. Like Mary, wherever we go and whatever we do, we carry Jesus with us into the space where we live our lives, and we carry him into the lives of others. And other people bring Jesus to us – the members of our community, members of our family and the circle of our friends and acquaintances, the people we seek to serve, even those whom we meet casually. This is true especially in the context of service; for wherever people seek to serve one another in self-forgetfulness, Jesus is especially present. Like Elizabeth, we need to develop the ability to recognise that deeper dimension; we need to be alert; we need to foster that gentle sensitivity to God's presence. We are called to recognise like Moses that the ground on which we tread is Holy Ground;[94] we are always in the heart of God. We are called to be everyday contemplatives.

In recent years there has been amongst all kinds of people a growing awareness of the value of silence, and of the need for a quieter, less active form of prayer. We can just sit still in the presence of God. We need not say anything or think anything or make special efforts. And God is not *out there*, but dwells deep within us in the still centre of our being. This is another journey, a journey of discovery well worth embarking upon.[95]

The Magnificat

The Gospel reading for today picks up Mary's response to Elizabeth's words of blessing, as she breaks into a hymn of praise, a hymn immortalised in the evening prayer of the Church. This creates a lull in the narrative movement which enables Luke to highlight the significance of what has so far taken place.

> And Mary said, *My soul magnifies the Lord, and my spirit rejoices in God my Saviour, for he has looked with favour on the lowliness of his servant. Surely, from now on all generations will call me blessed; for the Mighty One has done great things for me, and holy is his name. His mercy is for those who fear him from generation to generation. He has shown strength with his arm; he has scattered the proud in the thoughts of their hearts. He has brought down the powerful from their thrones, and lifted up the lowly; he has filled the hungry with good things, and sent the rich away empty. He has helped his servant Israel, in remembrance of his mercy, according to the promise he made to our ancestors, to Abraham and to his descendants for ever.* And Mary remained with her for about three months and then returned to her home. (Luke 1:46-56)

The Magnificat, as this hymn or canticle is usually called,[96] bears a close resemblance to the psalms of the Hebrew Bible commonly referred to as hymns of praise; it exhibits the kind of parallelism which is a feature of Jewish poetry. These hymns usually take the form of an introduction in which God is praised; a body, in which are listed the motives for praise (deeds which God has done for Israel and/or for the individual, and some of God's attributes); and a conclusion which may recapitulate the motives for praise, take the form of a blessing, or contain a request.

The language of the Magnificat is heavily influenced by the Hebrew Bible, and especially the song of rejoicing uttered by Hannah after giving her son Samuel to the Lord at the Shiloh Temple.[97] The hymn also introduces some key Lucan themes. By way of introduction, Mary celebrates and rejoices in her Lord and God as Saviour. The first two lines are in poetic parallelism: *My soul magnifies, my spirit rejoices*; the phrases mean simply *I magnify, I rejoice*. This is the first mention of the theme of salvation, which is central to the Gospel of Luke. The angel later proclaims to the shepherds that, *A saviour is born to you in the city of David.* Simeon, as he holds the child Jesus in his arms, joyfully acknowledges that, *My eyes have seen your salvation.*[98] The apostles will later preach the coming of salvation through the death and resurrection of Jesus; Luke links it here with the child's birth.[99] In this opening verse it is God who is proclaimed as Saviour, and Mary manifests a profound sense of God having freely gifted her. Mary's delight and rejoicing expresses the awareness that a new age is beginning.[100]

Following the usual pattern in this kind of hymn, she explains the reasons for her rejoicing. Initially, she focuses on what God has done for her personally. Her joy stems from God looking with loving care upon her lowly, powerless condition, her humble state as a young woman from rural Galilee, her poverty of spirit. Mary is thus associated with those figures in Israel's past who were poor and needy, and also with oppressed Israel as a whole. She sees herself as God's servant, confirming her statement to Gabriel earlier. She is aware that as a result of God's graciousness, all future generations will follow Elizabeth in acknowledging her blessedness.[101] This is because of her central role in the coming of salvation through her son. For Fitzmyer this verse expresses a fundamental attitude toward the believing Mother of the Lord.[102]

As the hymn evolves, Mary celebrates three of God's attributes: God is almighty; God is holy; God is merciful. Firstly, God is the Mighty One. The kind of powerful intervention witnessed in military acts of salvation in the past, especially in the Exodus, has been experienced by Mary, for the power of the Most High, for whom nothing is impossible, has overshadowed her.[103]

133

God's name, secondly, is acclaimed as holy; later Jesus will be recognised as the embodiment of God's holiness.[104] Mary knows this already because she has been told that he will be conceived through the Holy Spirit, and will be called holy. Mary, thirdly, acknowledges that God doing great things for her stems from his mercy and compassion, his gracious faithfulness towards all those who are open to Him. This has been true for countless generations right up to the time of her experience. What God has done in the past, God continues to do. In Jesus, God's compassion and mercy are present, and His loving faithfulness will establish a new covenant.

The motives for praising God now become less personally those of Mary, as the angle of focus widens. The thought is carried forward by a series of parallel antitheses.[105] The arrogant, conceited, haughty and self-confident are routed; this is probably in antithesis to the earlier *those who fear the Lord.* Princes are dethroned; the lowly and oppressed are raised up high. The starving are filled, whereas the rich are dismissed with empty hands. Such arrogance, pride, power and wealth are forms which opposition to God constantly takes and which God in His mercy combats. The adult Jesus will encounter them in his ministry.[106] This pattern of reversal, God's action in preferring the marginalised and the poor and needy, is a pattern or theme which will be evident during the ministry of Jesus.

The Greek *aorist* past tense is used in these verbs. In the context it seems unlikely that this should simply refer to what God has done in the past, as recorded in the Old Testament. Some scholars suggest that it is *a prophetic aorist*: Mary is predicting what will come about in the future through the child who is to be born. Her experience is a paradigm of what will happen for others who are poor. God has taken decisive action in the sending of his son, and Mary foresees as an accomplished fact the results which will follow in his mission.[107] Others believe that it is a *gnomic aorist*, which should therefore be translated in the present, and which describes God's normal way of proceeding. Alternatively, it is possible that the Magnificat is actually vocalising the sentiments of the Jewish Christians, proclaiming God's saving action through the death and resurrection of Jesus. [108]

The hymn draws to a conclusion by explicitly recalling God's faithful love shown to Abraham, the father of Israel, and to his descendants throughout history; God's constant faithfulness to the Covenant promise.[109] It is in this context of the Covenant and God's faithful love that God has once more come to the help of Israel, God's servant or child, in the event that has begun in Mary.[110] The canticle ends as it began with this reference to God's saving/helping. This new, definitive helping/saving intervention has begun in the conception of Jesus; Mary can therefore proclaim its fulfilment.

After Mary's canticle response to Elizabeth's acknowledgement of her role, Luke picks up the storyline. Mary remains in Judah's hill country for three months, and then returns to her own home.[111] The implication seems to be that she leaves prior to the birth of Elizabeth's child. From the historical point of view this would seem unlikely and unhelpful, unless she needed to go to Joseph's home because of her own pregnancy. However, the ending of the episode is dictated by literary considerations, for Luke requires that Mary should leave the scene before he narrates the birth of John, so as to preserve the balance of the two coming birth scenes in which only the two parents will be present.[112] The two women and the two stories go their separate ways as Mary departs for home.

On Lucan Hymns

The *Magnificat* is the first in a series of hymns, sometimes called canticles or psalms, found in Luke's Infancy Narrative.[113] The others are the *Benedictus* and the *Nunc Dimittis*, spoken by Zechariah and Simeon respectively, and the *Gloria in Excelsis* sung by the angelic choir at Jesus' birth; all of them form part of our current liturgical prayer.

Most scholars would maintain that none of the speakers proclaiming the three more substantial hymns (Mary, Zechariah, or Simeon) actually composed them historically. This was the pre-critical view based on the belief that the Infancy Narratives were derived from family circles. The hymns have a common style and a poetic polish which would argue against on-the-spot composition by three quite separate individuals. There are also some lines which do not suit individual speakers.

Therefore, some critics have suggested that the hymns were composed by Luke himself. This view has not been widely accepted, mainly because in that case one would expect to find a more uniform style and a smoother transition between narrative text and hymn. It has been observed that the narrative would flow easily without them. The more widely held view is that Luke has taken over already existing compositions and inserted them into his narrative with some additions and adaptations. The differences between the hymns suggest different original authorship within the same environment.

The hymns are composed in a Jewish poetic style and with an outlook thought to be typical of the period between 200BC and AD 100. They resemble a mosaic constructed from pieces taken from earlier poetry, from Old Testament and inter-testamental passages. It is unclear whether they were originally composed in Hebrew or Greek. It has even been suggested that Luke took them from a collection which had nothing to do with Christianity at all, similar to material in 1 Maccabees and the Qumran literature, and applied their sentiments to the situation of the speakers in his narrative.[114] The mainstream view maintains that they are probably early Jewish Christian hymns (there is little openness to Gentiles) celebrating the saving action of God through Jesus the Messiah. There is a strong tone of salvation accomplished. Their Christology is phrased in Old Testament terms, unlike the hymns in Paul. Luke saw that they could be introduced into the Infancy Narrative without much adaptation, because the piety and concept of salvation, expressed there, corresponds to that of the people in the narrative. Motifs already in the narrative are continued.[115]

Perhaps the hymns originated in a community, composed by different authors with the same background, possibly Christian Anawim. Brown maintains that these were people who, though perhaps materially poor, could not trust in their own strength but had to rely in utter confidence upon God – the lowly, the poor, the sick, the downtrodden, the widows and orphans. In post-exilic times the Anawim regarded themselves as the ultimate remnant of Israel. The Qumran community can be thought of as a sectarian group of Anawim, which split from the Maccabaeans. They evince features which are common to Anawim thought, though they also are quite different. Their psalms and hymns are very close in style to the Lucan canticles.

Brown thinks that it is not far-fetched to suggest that Luke got his canticles from a community of Jewish Anawim who had been converted to Christianity, a group that unlike the sectarians at Qumran would have continued to reverence the Temple and whose messianism was Davidic.[116]

They may have found in Jesus the fulfilment of their expectations, and used hymns to celebrate what God had accomplished in him. The Magnificat and Benedictus make sense in such a setting. Luke applied these general expressions of joy over the salvation brought in Jesus to the more specific setting of the Infancy. The characters embodied the piety of the Anawim. Brown concludes that the canticles come to us in Luke with a background of two levels of Christian meaning: the original general jubilation of the Christian converts among the remnant of Israel, the *Poor Ones* who recognised that, in Jesus, God had raised them up and saved them according to His promises; and the particular jubilation of a character in the infancy drama of salvation who is portrayed as a representative of the *Poor Ones*.[117] Perhaps they stem from the original Jewish Christian community in Jerusalem.

Reflections

The hymn which Luke places on Mary's lips in the Gospel narrative strongly echoes the hymn which Hannah pronounced after presenting her newly weaned child Samuel to Eli in the Shiloh Temple, which is used as the responsorial psalm for today's liturgy. Mary praises God above all as saviour. She is aware of the wonders God has wrought in her and the ongoing impact this will have on the world. As we join her in praying this canticle, perhaps we too can sharpen our awareness of all that God has done for us personally, and for our families, communities and our wider world. God's saving love continues to touch us in so many ways. And through us God's love has impacted the lives of others.

Mary moves on to praise the qualities most strongly associated with Israel's God, especially God's faithful love and compassionate mercy. This has been characteristic of God's dealings with Israel since the beginning. It will continue to be God's characteristic style until the end. The God of Luke's infancy story is essentially a God who is compassionate and faithful. As the story of Jesus continues during his ministry, it is clear that the God he reveals in words and actions is the God of compassionate love. This is the God with whom we need to get in touch this Advent and Christmastide.

An aspect of the hymn which we can overlook is Mary's description of the way in which God turns the world upside-down, reversing situations of injustice and oppression. The salvation, which God in His compassion brings, entails social and political change and reformation. In the 1980s the Guatemalan government forbade the public recitation of the Magnificat because of its revolutionary potential.[118] So, praying the Magnificat is demanding; it requires of us a heart which will be sensitive to the situations of the hungry, the lowly, the weak, the powerless; a heart which will enable us to be present and to stay alongside those in need, and work for the overturning of situations of oppression, untruth and injustice. It is a prayer which calls for action, because it celebrates the saving action of a compassionate God. Through us that love must continue to transform our world into the Kingdom.

December 23rd

The Birth and Naming of The Baptist

After the diptych of the two annunciation stories, Luke presents us with another diptych in the stories of the birth and naming of John and then of Jesus.[119] The latter passage, of course, does not form part of our Advent readings, which are the liturgical preparation for Christmas. Our Advent journey concludes with the birth and naming of John, and then with the Benedictus hymn proclaimed by Zechariah.

> Now the time came for Elizabeth to give birth, and she bore a son. Her neighbours and relatives heard that the Lord had shown his great mercy to her, and they rejoiced with her.
>
> On the eighth day they came to circumcise the child, and they were going to name him Zechariah after his father. But his mother said, *No; he is to be called John.* They said to her, *None of your relatives has this name.* Then they began motioning to his father to find out what name he wanted to give him. He asked for a writing-tablet and wrote, *His name is John.* And all of them were amazed. Immediately his mouth was opened and his tongue freed, and he began to speak, praising God. Fear came over all their neighbours, and all these things were talked about throughout the entire hill country of Judea. All who heard them pondered them and said, *What then will this child become?*
>
> For, indeed, the hand of the Lord was with him.
>
> (Luke 1:57-66)

The storyline proceeds in two stages with a week's gap in between. The angel's promise, which was first fulfilled in the conception of the child, now reaches further precise fulfilment in his birth.[120]

Naturally, Elizabeth, the focus of our attention, is overjoyed by the birth of her child and by the restoration of her honour in the community. She is joined in her rejoicing on both counts by her neighbours and relatives, who recognise that the Lord had lavished on her *His faithful love*. Such a joyful atmosphere fulfils the word of the angel to Zechariah concerning the impact of the birth of his future child. Luke reminds us that all that is taking place stems from God's free initiative, God's faithfulness and merciful love.

A week later, as was customary in accordance with the Law,[121] the time comes for the child to be circumcised and thus incorporated into membership of Israel, and to receive his name. The neighbours and relatives gather for the occasion. The head of the household usually performed the ceremony in the presence of a number of witnesses, and there was a prayer of blessing. The naming of the child normally took place shortly after birth, rather than a week later, which was a Greek custom. There are instances in the Old Testament of women naming their child, but by New Testament times it was generally the father who did so. It was traditional in priestly circles to name the child after his grandfather, but there are examples of the father's name being used, as in this case. The relatives have the intention of calling him Zechariah; perhaps they were already doing so.[122] Elizabeth, however, firmly insists that he be called John, which means *God's gracious gift*. For the mother he is indeed a gift from the gracious God; he is also a gift for his people. Without being aware of it, Elizabeth has chosen the name imposed by the angel.[123]

A woman's word in a patriarchal society counted for little, so those present persist in their intention, reminding Elizabeth that she is contravening the custom. Bypassing her, they appeal by means of signs to the child's deaf and dumb father. Zechariah requests a writing tablet, a wooden board coated with wax. Without having heard what his wife has said, he writes unequivocally that his name is (already) John, and thus he obeys Gabriel's injunction. The neighbours react with astonishment, probably at the confirmation of this unexpected name for his son.[124]

Some commentators feel that Luke wishes to imply that both parents acted without prior consultation or communication, under the inspiration of God, though according to our logic it is hard to believe that Zechariah would not have already informed his wife of this by writing! Zechariah's speech suddenly returns, for he has shown that he no longer wishes to be in control, that he is content to follow the Lord's command. His immediate reaction is to praise God, who is so clearly at work in all that is happening.

As a result of all that has occurred, the neighbours are filled with awe and fear at the obvious presence of the supernatural in the twofold miracle, and the news spreads like wildfire throughout the area, and provides the topic of conversation for some time. Those who hear what has happened treasure it in their hearts, and they wonder what this child will turn out to be.[125] The reader already has some idea of the eventual denouement. The narrator adds a comment which expresses the thought behind their questioning: *And indeed the hand of the Lord was with him.* These words convey the wider significance of the occasion, and communicate the assurance of God's accompanying power and guidance. The comment rounds off the scene on a note of hope and anticipation.[126]

Reflections

This reading, in its warm, realistic humanity, gives us much to ponder. The naming of a child can be an exciting or fraught event. There are personal preferences and family traditions to be accounted for. Whatever the reasons for a particular choice, the name we are given is ours for life. It both links us with our family history, and defines our individual and unique identity. I was baptised *Michael Thomas.* I think *Michael* because Mum and Dad liked the name; *Thomas* because my paternal grandfather and my mother's favourite uncle had that name.

I've never been fond of the *Thomas* bit, though it has proved useful as a way of distinguishing me from a fellow Salesian of my vintage called *Michael Winstanley,* without the *Thomas,* though most people adopted *big* and *little* to differentiate us!

Most names get abbreviated; for many friends I'm *Mike*, and I like that. *Mick* has always been unacceptable! A number of my friends with two Christian names are known by the second rather than the first. Names provide a fascinating topic for discussion! For me the most important aspect is the uniqueness of my identity in relation to others and to God. The great medieval philosopher/theologian, Duns Scotus, used to speak about the *thisness* (haecceitas) of things. Each blade of grass, each pebble on a beach is utterly unique. Much more so is a human being.

The question of the elderly couple's neighbours and friends, *What then will this child become?* echoes across centuries and cultures. It encapsulates unspoken hopes and dreams. It also captures something of life's unpredictability, fragility and mystery. It acknowledges that we are not entirely in control of our destiny. For a Christian family it is an invitation to make space for God in life's unfolding, and to trust in God's providential love: *Into your hands, O Lord, we commend our little son/daughter, your gracious gift to us. We humbly and gratefully believe that the hand of the Lord will be with our child, now and always.*

For Luke, this story illustrates God's faithfulness to His promises, His trustworthiness, and this is important as the story of Jesus develops later. It also manifests God's remarkable ability to surprise, to operate outside the box, to turn experience and expectations upside down. That too is a pattern which will recur later in the narrative.

The Benedictus

The final episode of Luke's story for Advent presents us with the hymn proclaimed by Zechariah when his voice returns. Known as the Benedictus, it is used daily in the Church's Morning Prayer.[127]

> Then his father Zechariah was filled with the Holy Spirit and spoke this prophecy: *Blessed be the Lord God of Israel, for he has looked favourably on his people and redeemed them. He has raised up a mighty saviour for us in the house of his servant David, as he spoke through the mouth of his holy prophets from of old, that we would be saved from our enemies and from the hand of all who hate us. Thus he has shown the mercy promised to our ancestors, and has remembered his holy covenant, the oath that he swore to our ancestor Abraham, to grant us that we, being rescued from the hands of our enemies, might serve him without fear, in holiness and righteousness before him all our days. And you, child, will be called the prophet of the Most High; for you will go before the Lord to prepare his ways, to give knowledge of salvation to his people by the forgiveness of their sins. By the tender mercy of our God, the dawn from on high will break upon us, to give light to those who sit in darkness and in the shadow of death, to guide our feet into the way of peace.* (Luke 1:67-80)

On the eighth day after the birth of John, the naming and circumcision ceremony is held. As this draws to a conclusion, with the neighbours fearful and wondering about the child's future, Zechariah is filled with the Holy Spirit, and bursts into a prophetic hymn of praise.[128] In some ways Zechariah is also providing an answer to the people's pensive pondering, with which the previous scene concluded.

143

The positioning of the canticle here rather than after verse 64, where mention is made of his prayerful outburst, means that it has a place of emphasis. It also points forward to the story which follows as the Gospel unfolds, carrying the theological weight of the narrative.[129]

The canticle closely resembles traditional Old Testament psalms or hymns of praise, called *berakah*. It commences by blessing or praising the God of Israel, and then in two balanced strophes provides the reasons for such praise. There is a lengthy insertion which is addressed directly to the child. This is followed by the original recapitulating conclusion.[130]

The opening blessing, *Blessed be the Lord God of Israel,* is a stereotyped formula frequently found in the psalms.[131] In this way a link is made with Israel's past, especially the Exodus event, in a hymn which will celebrate God's new redemptive intervention through Jesus. Reference to God as the God of Israel has an exclusive ring, discounting the Gentiles.

Two reasons for praising God are put forward in parallel: His visiting His people, and His raising up a saviour. Firstly, God is praised for having *visited* His people. The idea of God's *visiting* is used in the Hebrew Bible with reference both to God's judging and, especially, to His saving interventions on behalf of His people;[132] it is an important idea for Luke.[133] The nature of God's *visitation* is clearly specified here as being redemptive, liberating, delivering. The verbs throughout this section are in the past tense, indicating an accomplished fact, but, building on what God has achieved in Israel's past, they refer to God's liberating work already begun with the birth of the child and the conception of the Messiah. Though not yet finally accomplished, God has set in motion the train of events which will achieve such deliverance.[134]

The means of such redemption consists in God establishing for the people a horn of salvation, or mighty saviour, or a saving power, who is the Davidic Messiah.[135] This is the second reason for Zechariah praising God. The image is derived from the upright horns of a bull or ox, later transferred to the horns on a victorious warrior's helmet.[136] It is a symbol of power and strength.

The image fits the idea of a triumphant messianic king.[137] In doing so, God is fulfilling what God promised in ancient times through the prophets, and in this way a long line of preparation is brought to completion.[138] The content of these promises was the saving of the people from their enemies, again using poetic parallelism, *from the hands of those who hate us.*[139] In the psalms such enemies can be personal or pagan foes. In this way God shows His mercy and faithful love, keeping the solemn covenant promise made to the fathers of old.

The second strophe highlights the covenant attributes of mercy or loving kindness in choosing Israel, and faithfulness to the choice made, despite the inadequacies of human beings. These are two key characteristics of God which were highlighted also in the Magnificat. Here the emphasis moves away from David and the promises made to him, for the covenant explicitly recalled is that made to Abraham, which in the eyes of the early Christians was wider and more fundamental than the Mosaic covenant.[140] *The salvation that is now coming from Yahweh, in raising his horn in David's house, is seen as an extension of his covenant promises to Israel's ancestors of long ago.*[141] The purpose of this covenant oath is here described in terms of deliverance from the hands of enemies and freedom from the fear of persecution, so that they might serve God in holiness and upright living or justice forever, qualities which ought to characterise the covenanted people.[142] Whilst the ideas of service and worship have a cultic and liturgical ring, they embrace a whole way of living.[143]

At this point the style of the hymn alters, as Zechariah turns to his child and addresses him directly. Such a switch is not uncommon in Jewish literature. It is thought that Luke is responsible for the addition of these verses to the original hymn. In words which echo the message of Gabriel earlier, Zechariah celebrates the role which his son will fulfil in the unfolding of God's saving intervention. John too will be a prophet of God the Most High, announcing God's new salvation.[144]

He will exercise this role by going before the Lord in order to prepare his way; God's visitation takes the form of the coming of Jesus.[145] This is, in fact, how the ministry of John the Baptiser is later described in the Gospel narrative.[146]

The next sentence is in parallel: the Lord's way is prepared through John providing the people with the knowledge of salvation, a salvation which consists in the forgiveness of sins. Knowledge of salvation here does not refer to something intellectual; it means that salvation is personally experienced deep within through the forgiveness of sins. In his later ministry, John proclaims a baptism for the forgiveness of sins, and offers teaching on how different groups of people should live.[147] Forgiveness is central to the message and ministry of Jesus too; it is a key Lucan concept throughout the Gospel and Acts.[148]

As is usually the case, the final verses of the hymn summarise the ideas already expressed. The source of all that takes place is the faithful mercy of God, God's loving compassion. Such compassion brings about the visitation from above of a figure described as *the dawn from on high, to give light.* The key word in Greek can mean a growing shoot, branch, or a rising star, which are both messianic images.[149] Perhaps this twofold significance is intended. The term was used amongst Greek-speaking Jews to describe the expected Davidic king. Some manuscripts have a future verb, *will come*, others a past, *has come.*[150] The Messiah comes as a source of light and liberation *for those sitting in darkness and the shadow of death,*[151] a light to guide our feet into the way of peace.[152] The theme of peace is taken up again later in the hymn of the angels at the birth of Jesus. This image balances the horn of salvation imagery found earlier in the canticle, with its possible implications of force and political might.[153] In the Old Testament, salvation has to do mainly with the overthrowing of Israel's enemies, whereas for Luke it concerns liberation from sin.

According to this canticle, the main reason for blessing God is what God has done for His people in Jesus the Messiah. In the period of Old Testament preparation, promises were made to David and his descendants through the prophets, and a covenant oath to Abraham and his descendants. The hymn concludes with a eulogy of Jesus, and is therefore Christological. John the Baptiser is the bridge between old and new. [154]

After the hymn, which closes by pointing to the coming Messiah, the narrative is briefly resumed, and the section which deals with John is brought to a conclusion. John is removed from the scene before Luke moves on to concentrate his attention on the birth of Jesus. The boy John is said to grow physically, and also to develop in spirit before the Lord. The phrasing is stereotyped, and echoes many of the parallels which have run through this opening chapter: Isaac, Samson, Samuel.[155] The child goes off into the Judean desert and lives in the seclusion of the wilderness until the moment when he inaugurates his prophetic mission to Israel. As usual the scene thus ends on a note of departure. John's story is taken up again in 3:2 when the word of God came to John, the son of Zechariah, in the desert, and he embarks on his ministry.[156]

Reflections

Under the influence of the Holy Spirit the second great hymn of Luke's Infancy Narrative is spoken by John's father Zechariah. The Spirit has already touched Mary and Elizabeth, and will be active later in the story when Simeon and Anna meet the child in the Temple. The traditional format of the canticle gives way to Zechariah's vision of his son's future role in God's saving visitation of our world. Parents often wonder what their children will become when grown up; Zechariah has a clear vision of his son's role and in sharing it, he provides answers to the neighbours' pondering.

In the process of outlining John's mission, he also highlights salient aspects of the role of the one for whom he will prepare. Jesus will be a source of light for those who sit in darkness and in the shadow of death. These words which have an Isaian resonance recur in Matthew's Gospel as Jesus leaves Nazareth and makes his home in Capernaum at the start of his ministry. The occasions when Jesus heals blind people illustrate his light-bringing.

His teaching scatters much shadow and darkness, for Jesus is the great revealer. Through his healing, teaching, and his way of living and relating, he revealed to the people who encountered him the face of God, a God of forgiveness and compassion, a God who wanted to share their lives, a God of faithful love. He revealed to them a set of values and attitudes which mirror something of that God. He revealed to them the contours of a different world which he called God's Kingdom.

In the course of our Advent journey centuries later we have probably been drawn to acknowledge the areas of shadow and darkness in our minds, in our lives and in our wider world. We have been exposed to Jesus' words and have had the opportunity to reflect on his message and healing ministry. In and through it all we have been able to encounter the God whom Jesus reveals. The core of Jesus' message is that God loves each of us very deeply, with a love that will always be there. God walks with us on our journey. God waits to welcome us in His embrace. Perhaps during these weeks we have become more aware of God's presence deep within our heart, and have been able to surrender to God's love a little more. It is that love which bursts into our world with gentle power at Christmas.

Endnotes

1. See Gen 6:14-25; Ezra 2:62-63; Neh 7:64-65
2. Gal 4:4; in Romans 1:3 he writes: descended from David according to the flesh.
3. In the 90s, and therefore at a time proximate to the writing of this Gospel, the famous Jewish historian Josephus provides his own genealogy, linking himself to priestly and royal lines. For the Infancy Narratives, in addition to the bibliography mentioned for Matthew and Luke in chapter one, see especially R.E.Brown, *The Birth of the Messiah* (London, Doubleday 1993); *A Coming Christ in Advent* (Collegeville, Liturgical Press 1988); *An Adult Christ at Christmas* (Collegeville, Liturgical Press 1978); also M.J. Borg & J.D. Crossan, *The First Christmas* (*HarperCollins*, New York 2007); J. Corley ed., *New Perspectives on the Nativity* (London, T&T Clark 2009); also Dunn, *Jesus Remembered* (Eerdmans, Cambridge 2003), p.340-348; F.J. Moloney, *Beginning the Good News* (Homebush, St Paul Publications 1992), p.73-100; *The Living Voice of the Gospel* (Dublin, Veritas 2006), p.127-162.
4. Matthew's community was composed of convert Jews and Gentiles; from the outset and throughout his Gospel he has this mixed constituency in mind. Reference to Abraham, in whom all the nations of the world were blessed, is early evidence of this (see Gen 12:3; 17:4). Borg & Crossan, p.25-53, maintain that the Infancy Narratives are neither fact nor fable; they are best understood as parable and overture, rich in theological significance, and a summary of what is to follow.
5. The first reading for today, from Gen 49:2,8-10, highlights the role of Judah.

6. W. Carter, *Matthew 1-2 and Roman Political Power*, in *New Perspectives on the Nativity*, p.80-81, points out that the exile was understood theologically as a punishment; later Babylon is judged by God for its oppression, and its empire is ended by Cyrus, acting as God's instrument. The situation in Matthew's day is analogous and the reader is meant to draw a parallel. The Roman imperialists have destroyed Jerusalem and its temple, and this can be understood as God's punishment of Judaism (21:45; 22:7), but God will similarly overcome Rome and establish His rule.

7. Viviano, 'Making Sense of the Matthaean Genealogy: 1:17 and the Theology of History', in *New Perspectives on the Nativity*, p.100 and 109, notes the view that the missing 14th name in the third section of the genealogy is Jesus as the future coming Son of Man, which is a divine title.

8. Beare, p.63. For a detailed reflection on this approach to history, see Viviano, p.91-109. He sees Matthew's threefold structure as a partial outline of a common seven part scheme of biblical periodisation of which he was aware.

9. Meier, *Matthew*, p.4; Davies & Allison accept this view. Borg & Crossan, p.88, speak of *parabolic mathematics*.

10. Wright, 1:3.

11. For details see Brown, *Birth*, p.71-74; Moloney, *Living Voice*, p.132-133.

12. They were not, however, presented as sinners in the biblical tradition. For further information concerning the women, see Borg & Crossan, p.89-93.

13. Brown, *Birth*, p.74; also Borg & Crossan, p.92. On p.96-98 they consider that the genealogies in both Gospels are intended also to counter the genealogy of the Roman Emperor Augustus.

14. See Brown, *Birth*, 123-124.

15. Brown, *Coming Christ*, p.29-30, notes the view sometimes proposed that Joseph realised that the pregnancy was through the Spirit, and so wished to divorce Mary because he felt unworthy of the relationship. Another view suggests that Mary was so holy that Joseph would have assumed

that the pregnancy was of God. Brown rejects these views, observing that the point of the angelic annunciation is to reveal the origin of the pregnancy. Borg & Crossan, p.101-110, wonder why Joseph presumed that there was an issue of adultery (which is not a problem in Luke). For them the idea stems from popular traditions concerning the conception of Moses, which contain the elements of divorce, prophecy and remarriage.

16. Deut 22:20-21.

17. Brown, *Birth*, p.155-159. We shall find an excellent example in tomorrow's reading.

18. This is the only instance in the New Testament when someone other than Jesus is called by this title. 2 Sam 7:12-13 reads: *I will raise up your son after you...I will make his royal throne firm forever.*

19. In fact the angel tells Joseph: *you are to name him Jesus.*

20. Brown, *Coming Christ*, p.36.

21. Brown, *Birth*, p.131. Matthew's Jesus later calls the people *My Church* (16:18). Cabrido, p.129, stresses that in the OT *laos* is a specific term for a specific people.

22. Byrne, p.24; see also 9:8; 18:12-35; 20:28; 26:28. Cabrido, p.128, notes that the reader is reminded of God's saving activity throughout Israel's history. Carter, p.82, maintains that the fact that the name Jesus is linked with Joshua suggests that his saving task is much more extensive than only personal and individual sins. The imperial power of the Assyrians is evoked by the quotation from Isaiah, and this is currently paralleled by the Romans. Such *evoking of imperial powers indicates that the extent of Jesus' saving commission is to restore all of human life to participate in God's good and just purposes.*

23. Senior, p.41.

24. Moloney, *Living Voice*, p.136, observes that Matthew looks back to the Old Testament as an explanation of what God does through Jesus; this is an indication of a largely Jewish community that looked to the scriptures to explain their new situation as Christians. Borg & Crossan, p.202, stress that in their original context none of the five infancy scriptural passages is a prediction of the distant future of Jesus.

25. Davies & Allison, p.16: There is no evidence that Judaism understood the quotation messianically.

26. The Hebrew says *she will call*; the Greek *you will call*. Matthew changes it to *they will call*, widening the audience.

27. The virginal conception is a feature of the Infancy Narratives of both Matthew and Luke, and is probably earlier tradition. Borg & Crossan, p.120, see it as an exaltation of the New Testament over the Old, and to counter the story of the divine conception of Augustus. *Mary's divine conception is different from and greater than all others.* For the pre-enlightenment world, a divine conception was their way of asserting an individual's transcendental character.

28. In Judaism paternity was based on the man's acknowledgement of the child by giving it a name. Legal paternity was understood as real paternity. By exercising this right Joseph, son of David, becomes the legal father of Jesus, (legal is a more exact term than foster or adoptive), and in this way the child of Mary is drawn into the line of David. Joseph's role in Matthew's story is more important than that of Mary; she does not speak or receive any revelation. Joseph is mentioned 8 times in Matthew, 3 times in Luke; Mary 3 and 11 times respectively. The text states: *he had no marital relations with her until she had borne a son.* This gives no information about the marital situation after the birth, since that was not Matthew's concern. (See Brown, *Birth*, p.132).

29. Mark 14:8

30. For bibliography on Luke see Tuesday of Week One; for the Infancy Narrative see Dec 17th.

31. Brown, *Birth*, p.264, suggests this structure: 1:5-7: Introduction of the *dramatis personae*; 1:8-23: Annunciation by the angel; (8-10, Setting; 11-20, Core; 21-23 Conclusion); 1:24-25: Epilogue. Green, p.67, suggests a chiastic pattern to 8-23. Scholars note the semitic character and septuagint language of the narrative.

32. Marshall, p.51, opts for 40; McBride, p.22; Green, p.62; Fitzmyer, 1:321, for 37.

33. Herod was noted for building programmes, tyranny, and attempts at Hellenisation.

34. The only Elizabeth mentioned in the Hebrew Bible was the wife of Aaron (Exod.6:23).

35. Johnson, p.32, observes that these characteristics reflect the simple piety associated with the *poor of Yahweh*, the *Anawim*, people who trust in God and are open to revelation.

36. Lev 20:20; Gen 16:4; 29:32; 30:1; 1 Sam 1:5-6; Psa 127:3-5; 128. Green, p.63, notes the dissonance between blamelessness and lack of blessedness. Brown, *Birth*, p.268, states the couple combine priestly origins and the blameless observance of the Law, and are for Luke representatives of the best in the religion of Israel.

37. Zechariah's reply (1:18) is identical with that of Abraham (Gen 15:8); Elizabeth's joy is reminiscent of that of Sarah (Gen 21:6). The similarities with the story of Elkanah and Hannah in 1 Sam include: the opening of the story introducing the characters; the Temple setting (Shiloh in their case) and sacrifice; Hannah's distress because of her barrenness; her prayer for a boy child, whom she would dedicate to God and who would be a Nazirite. Eli, the priest, assures her that her prayer will be granted. On their return home, she becomes pregnant. (See Brown, *Coming*, p.43-44). Luke's language and style deliberately recalls the Old Testament. These biblical episodes provide models for Luke's storytelling. Green, p.69, describes the Old Testament as a *data bank* for Luke, who has constructed a complex network of echoes. Brown, *Coming*, p.44, and *Birth*, p.270, notes that Luke recalls the Law, the Prophets, and the Wisdom traditions, thus covering the timespan of Matthew's genealogy. Borg & Crossan, p.212-213, note that Luke does not use the prediction-fulfilment formula we encountered in Matthew; he echoes phrases from the Hebrew scriptures in narrative and hymns.

38. 24:53

39. They numbered up to 18,000, and were divided into twenty-four groups or orders, named after the grandsons of Aaron; the Abijah section was eighth in the list. Only four of the original group of 24 had returned from the exile; they were redivided into 24 new groups and given the old names. Brown, *Birth*, p.258-259; McBride, p.23. For further details see Green, p.68; Marshall, p.54; Caird, p.50-51; Fitzmyer, 1:322.

40. Exod 30:7-8; 2 Chron 13:11. The only person who was allowed closer to the locus of God's presence was the High Priest who entered the Holy of Holies on the Day of Atonement.

41. In the Hebrew Bible there are several episodes in which the birth of a child is announced. These follow a similar pattern, a pattern which is found here, and also in the annunciation to Mary later. See Brown, *Birth*, p.156, Table VIII; he describes the template as follows: an appearance (or vision) of the Lord (or God's angel); a reaction of fear (or a prostration); the recipient is addressed, usually by name, and told not to fear; the message affirms that someone is or will be with child and will give birth; the name of the child is given (sometimes with an etymological explanation); the child's role and accomplishments are rehearsed; the visionary poses an objection or question, or asks for a sign. (See Gen 17&18 regarding Isaac; 16:7-15 regarding Hagar and Ishmael; Judges 13:3-20 regarding Samson, which is the first reading for Dec. 19th). Some vocation stories show similar features: the call of Gideon in Judges 6:12-23 and of Moses in Exod 3:2-12. The annunciation narrative is also influenced by Dan 8:16f; 9:21f; 10:8,12,15; here we find reference to Gabriel, a vision during evening liturgical prayer, fear, dumbness, the Holy of Holies. See also Evans, p.144. Fitzmyer, 1:309, 316-317, takes the view that Luke is using a Baptist source for this episode, a view which Brown resists (*Birth*, p.244-245, 265-279).

42. Brown, *Birth*, p.260. Evans, p.151, refers to the speculative theology of angels which developed in Judaism in the 2nd century in apocalyptic circles and popular piety. Some were given names. Unlike the Pharisees, the Sadducees rejected the innovation. For details of the Daniel links, see Brown, *Birth*, p.270-271.

43. Green, p.74; on p.73, he refers to a divine remembrance motif; God remembers and acts of behalf of certain people (see Gen 30:22; 1 Sam 1:11,19-20). Marshall, p.56, thinks it unlikely that Zechariah was praying for a personal request at that time, though he may have done so at other times; prayer for the salvation of Israel was associated with the evening

sacrifice. Brown, *Birth*, p.260, takes the opposite view.

44. Judg 13:4-14; Jer 35:1-11; Num 6:3; 1 Sam 1:9-15. Luke is linking John with Samuel and Samson. Abstinence from wine, cider and beer was associated with separation from normal life for a divine task, temporary (like officiating in the temple) or lifelong. Here it is indication of John's lifelong dedication to God. (See Green, p.75). For Marshall, p.57, John is simply described as an ascetic.

45. See Samson in Judg 16:17; 13:7, and Jeremiah in Jer 1:5,14. This is the first mention of the Spirit in Luke.

46. Mal 2:7; 3:1; 3:23; 4:5. In the original text the Lord refers to God; it probably does here, since Gabriel has not yet announced the coming of Jesus. Brown, *Birth*, p.273-274, notes how the language of these verses anticipates the descriptions of John found in the ministry (3:1-3; 7:27-28; 7:33; 20:6), an ascetic prophet calling upon Israel to repent. Fitzmyer, 1:327, notes that, contrary to the view of many, in pre-Christian literature Elijah is not presented as precursor of the Messiah.

47. This phrase is found in Mal 3:24 and Sir 48:10 regarding Elijah. The influence of Malachi on the text is significant, and communicates the coming of the end-time.

48. Brown, *Birth*, p.278-279, interprets this difficult parallelism as the fathers/ancestors are the disobedient; the (unexpected) children of Abraham, the Gentiles, find the Wisdom of God in Jesus (see 7:31-35). Marshall, p.60, favours the meaning of the restoring of good family relationships. Green, p.77, notes the image of God in the Gospel as a father caring for his children, and similar references to human fathers.

49. Johnson, p.35.

50. His question is the same as that of Abraham (Gen 15:8).

51. Gabriel in Dan 8-9 is entrusted by God to reveal divine mysteries. *Good News* recalls Isa 40-66, the coming final redemption.

52. Green, p.79-80; Marshall, p.60-61.

53. Byrne, p.22. The literary parallels with Daniel suggest dumbness as a sign.

54. There are clear echoes of 1 Sam 1:19-20. Green, p.63, observes that the spotlight shines brightest on Elizabeth: barren and disgraced at the outset, pregnant and restored to a position of honour at the close. On p.66, he comments that Elizabeth's having a child does not depend on Zechariah but on a miraculous intervention. The language of the text recalls Sarah's rejoicing (Gen 21:6), and Rachel's (Gen 30:22-23).

55. Brown, *Birth*, p.282; Marshall, p.62; Fitzmyer, 1:321.

56. McBride, p.24.

57. The word *parthenos* is twice used to describe her. It means a young unmarried girl. Johnson, p.36, holds that there are no implications concerning sexual experience, but Marshall, p.64; Green, p.86; Fitzmyer, 1:343, maintain that, following the LXX, there are strong implications of virginity. Green, p.85; Marshall, p.64, make a link with Isa 7:10-17; this is, incidentally, the passage chosen for today's first reading in the liturgy. Brown, *Birth*, p.300, does not find arguments making the link with the Isaian passage convincing. He notes that the Isaian terminology is found in other OT annunciation stories. Borg and Crossan, p.113-114, are also of the view that there is no evidence that Luke knows any connection between Mary's virginity and the Isaian text. Similarly, Fitzmyer, 1:336.

58. Brown, *Birth*, p.287; Fitzmyer, 1:344.

59. Deut 22:23-24.

60. Johnson, p.39. Byrne, p.22, writes that we have moved from the centre to the margins.

61. See Brown, *Birth*, table X, p.294, and table XI, p.297. Johnson, p.38, comments that because of the many parallels between this story and the previous angelic visitation, the points of difference are all the more striking: John is great before the Lord, Jesus is great and is Son; John will prepare the people, Jesus will rule them; John has a temporary role, Jesus' will last forever; John is a prophet, Jesus is Son; John is filled with the Spirit as a prophet, the Spirit overshadows Jesus and makes him the *Holy One*. Green, p.83-84, discusses the similarities and points of contrast between the 2 stories.

Brown, *Birth*, p.296, makes the point that the material not explained by the literary pattern requires attention: the (virginal) manner of conception, the description of the future accomplishments of the child, and the portrait of Mary in v 34 and 38. Close adherence to the literary form raises a question about the historicity of the stereotyped features.

62. See Zeph 3:14-15; Zech 9:9; Joel 2:21.

63. See Gen.26:24; 28:15; Ruth 2:4; Judges 6:12; Jer.1:8,19; 15:20. The phrase is a declaration, not a wish.

64. B.E.Reid, 'Prophetic Voices of Elizabeth, Mary and Anna in Luke 1-2', in *New Perspectives on the Nativity*, p.38, understands this scene as Mary's prophetic call. Like the great prophets Moses and Jeremiah, she is full of questions and fear, but receives God's reassurance.

65. Hagar (Gen 16:11), Leah (Gen 30:13), the mother of Samson (Judg 13:24), and the mother of Samuel (1 Sam 1:20).

66. *Most High* is frequent in the LXX, and is used of God by Luke in 6:35 and 8:28; Jesus' origins and role transcend those of John.

67. As Brown points out (*Birth*, p.310-311; *Coming*, p.64), the parallels between v.32-33 and 2 Sam 7:9-16 are very close, (see Isa 9:7; Psa 89:3); Mary's child will be the Davidic Messiah. Green, p.88, states that the connection with the expectation of a restored Davidic monarchy is unmistakable. Also Fitzmyer, 1:348.

68. Gen 46:27; Exod 19:3; Isa 8:17.

69. Byrne, p.23.

70. Many explanations of a psychological nature have been put forward to explain Mary's question. The best explanation, however, is literary: it is a feature of the usual pattern and it allows the angel to explain more about the child's identity. Luke's message is Christological. For details, see Brown, *Birth*, p.303-309; Fitzmyer, 1:348-350.

71. *The Holy Spirit* and *the power from the Most High* are synonymous. For Pentecost see Acts 1:8; see also Isa 32:15 and 1 Sam 16:13. Brown, *Birth*, p.311-316, notes that the language here (v35) also has links with that used of the

Davidic Messiah: the spirit comes upon the Davidic branch in Isa 11:1-2; the term holy is associated with the Davidic shoot in Isa 4:2-3; and there is a parallel between the Son of God and the Son of the Most High, which echo the sonship of David in Psa 2:7 and 2 Sam 7:14. The terminology is not, however, primarily that of OT prophecy, but that of NT preaching. The Spirit comes not on the Davidic king, but upon his mother. We are not dealing with the adoption by coronation as God's son, but the begetting of God's Son in the womb of Mary through God's creative Spirit without human intercourse. We are dealing with early Christian formulations of Christology, in which Jesus is acclaimed as God's Son; this was linked originally with the resurrection (see Rom 1:3-4: *born of the seed of David, designated Son of God in power according to the Spirit through the resurrection*), moved backwards into the ministry (especially in the baptism and transfiguration scenes), and now moved further backwards to the Infancy Narrative. See also Fitzmyer, 1:340.

72. Gen 1:2; Exod 40:35; Num 9:18,22; see Psa 91:4;140:7.

73. Byrne, p.24. McBride, p.25-26, notes that a virginal conception has no precedent in Jewish thought. Such a conception through the power of the Holy Spirit points to Jesus' unique status. Caird, p.52, points out that the OT was familiar with the concept of divine fatherhood (Israel, David). In Jesus' ministry he refers to God as *Father*, expressing an intimate relationship of which he was aware. Luke is telling us that Jesus entered upon this status of sonship at his birth by a new creative act of the Spirit.

74. Gen 18:14

75. Green, p.91. Marshall, p.71, notes that the term indicates a female relative, not necessarily a cousin; it may also suggest that Mary is of priestly descent. Also Fitzmyer, 1:352, 344.

76. Reid, *New Perspectives*, p.39, stresses the risk involved when a prophet says 'yes'. With Mary there is an undercurrent of upheaval and scandal, the problem of local suspicions, gossip, whisperings.

77. Brown, *Birth*, p.316-319, is of the opinion that Luke's portrait of Mary in this episode is shaped from his account of her in

the ministry, and is consistent with it, as in the case of John the Baptist in the previous episode. Similarly, Fitzmyer, 1:341.

78. McBride, p.27.
79. *Do not be afraid* introduces the message of the angel to the women at the empty tomb (Matt 28:5).
80. Mark 3:13-14.
81. Green, p.92.
82. Brown, *Birth*, p.331, 341. The phrase can also be translated as *with eagerness*.
83. The phrasing recalls 2 Sam 2:1. It was highly unusual for a young woman to wander round her own town unaccompanied, let alone take a lengthy journey. The idea of a journey is an important Lucan theme; journeys are often related to the fulfilment of God's purpose. See Green, p.95; N. King, 'The Significance of the Inn for Luke's Infancy Narrative' in *New Perspectives*, ed. J.Corley, p.71-73.
84. 1 Sam 1:1.
85. Gen 19:14; 22:3.
86. For LaVerdiere, p.23, in Mary the New Testament reaches out to the Old, transforms it, and gives it its ultimate significance.
87. Gen 25:22.
88. McBride, p.29; Byrne, p.25; Johnson, p.41; Brown, *Birth*, p.341.
89. The word used here is *eulogēmenos*, which is used to invoke on human beings the blessing of God; here the blessing has already been granted. (See Brown, *Birth*, p.333). The fact that it is Elizabeth who blesses Mary indicates Jesus' superiority over John. Fitzmyer, 1.364, reminds us that for the Jewish mind a woman's greatness was measured by the children she bore; Mary therefore surpasses all others.
90. Jdt 13:18: *Blessed are you, daughter,...among all women on earth*; in Judg 5:24, the prophet Deborah says: *Blessed among women be Jael*; in Deut 28:4, Moses tells the people: *Blessed shall be the fruit of your womb*. Elizabeth speaks likewise as a prophet; Mary too has a salvific role. (See also Reid, *New Perspectives*, p.40).

91. 2 Sam 6:9.

92. 2 Sam 24:21. Green, p.96, notes that in Mary's travelling to visit her relative, and greeting her first, social conventions are turned upside down, for she is the greater one. This foreshadows the way in which her son, though recognised as *Lord*, will live and serve.

93. Fitzmyer, 1:358.

94. Exod 3:5.

95. See, for instance, M. Laird, *Into the Silent Land* (London, DLT 2006); *A Sunlit Absence: Silence, Awareness, Contemplation* (New York, OUP 2011); B. O'Rourke, *Finding Your Hidden Treasure* (London, DLT 2011); F. Jalics, *The Contemplative Way* (New York, Paulist 2011); M.J. Cunningham, *A Connected Life* (Bolton, Don Bosco Publications 2014).

96. The Latin for *glorifies* or *magnifies*. Some scholars have suggested that this canticle is more appropriate on the lips of Elizabeth; but the manuscript evidence overwhelmingly favours Mary. See McBride, p.30; Caird, p.56; Johnson, p.41; Green, p.96; Marshall, p.78; Fitzmyer, 1:365-366. Brown, *Birth*, p.334-336, provides a detailed treatment of the issues involved.

97. 1 Sam 2:1-2; see also Hab 3:18; Sir 51:1; Psa 35:9. For details of Old Testament background, see Brown, *Birth*, Table XII; Fitzmyer, 1:356-357. Green, p.101, refers to the hymns of praise of Moses (Exod 15:1-18), Miriam (Exod 15:19-21), Deborah (Judg 5:1-31), Asaph (1 Chr 16:8-36) Judith (Jdt 16:1-17), as well as Hannah. In this way God's activity is extended into the past; what is happening in Mary's case is in continuity with the past.

98. 2:11; 2:30. Jesus later tells Zacchaeus: *today salvation has come to this house* (19:9). Also Acts 13:26; 28:28.

99. See Acts 13:26; 28:28.

100. Fitzmyer, 1:367.

101. See Leah in Gen 29:32; 30:13 and Hannah in 1 Sam 1:11.

102. Fitzmyer, 1:367.

103. 1:35,37. See Zeph 3:17. Acts 2:22; 10:38 recognises such power at work in Jesus' ministry.

104. Acts 3:14; 4:27,30.

105. See Hannah's canticle in 1 Sam 2:7-8. McBride, p.30, refers to the hymn of a Cinderella people. Brown, *Birth*, p.357, refers to Mary as the spokeswoman of the *Anawim*, the faithful remnant of Israel who put their trust and hope in God.

106. Green, p.104. Reid, *New Perspectives*, p.40, observes that it is on Mary's lips that Luke first articulates a vision for a new world order.

107. Caird, p.55. Marshall, p.84, suggests that what God has now begun to do, and Mary regards prophetically as already having come to fruition, is described in terms of what God actually did in OT times, as expressed in Israel's praise in the OT.

108. Brown, *Birth*, p.363. Luke is anticipating here the beatitudes and woes of the sermon on the plain (6:20-26). Throughout his Gospel he includes the teaching of Jesus emphasising that wealth and power are not the true values (see 12:16-19; 16:25-26; 21:1-4). Green, p.100, points out that the images of God's saving work are set within the larger narrative world of foreign occupation and religio-political oppression; Mary's vision of redemption should not be spiritualised as though unconnected with the social realities of daily existence. Also Marshall, p.85; Brown, *Birth*, p.363.

109. Mention of Abraham may suggest that God's saving presence could extend beyond Israel (see 3:8).

110. Johnson, p.42, translates v.54 as: he has taken Israel his child by the hand, remembering his mercy. On p.43, he notes that Mary has a representative and symbolic role for Israel.

111. Reid, *New Perspectives*, p.39, notes that it is not only a question of Mary helping Elizabeth; Elizabeth, the older woman who has lived with integrity and faithfulness despite the anguish and shame of being childless, also supports Mary like a wise mentor in these difficult days for her.

112. Brown, *Birth*, p.346, stresses that literary structure is far more important than the psychology of the characters involved; we are not dealing with family history but the dramatisation of the theology of salvation history. Fitzmyer, 1:362.

113. Brown, *Birth*, p.346-355.
114. Noted without agreement by McBride, p.28-29.
115. Borg & Crossan, p.213, see the hymns as pre-Lucan Christian canticles. Fitzmyer, 1:357 holds that the *Magnificat* is from a pre-Lucan Jewish Christian source.
116. Brown, *Birth*, p.352.
117. Brown, *Birth*, p.354.
118. Reid, *New Perspectives*, p.41.
119. With regard to the Baptist the emphasis is on the naming; with Jesus it is on the birth.
120. The description echoes Rebecca in Gen 25:24; the rejoicing recalls Sarah in Gen 21:6.
121. Circumcision was the sign of faithfulness to the covenant made by God with Abraham (Gen 17:9-14). It was enshrined in the Mosaic Law (Lev 12:3). The elderly couple are obedient.
122. The tense of the verb could be simple imperfect rather than conative (*they were trying to call*).
123. L.J. Maluf, Zechariah's Benedictus: *A New Look at a Familiar Text*, in *New Perspectives on the Nativity*, p.50, sees the neighbours clinging to the patterns of their past. The parents embrace what is new and heaven-inspired. Reid, p.42, notes that Luke does not say how Elizabeth knew the name; she is attuned to God, and this is a prophetic word.
124. Amazement and fear are typical reactions to the supernatural in Luke.
125. Zechariah will answer this question to some extent in the *Benedictus*.
126. Exod 6:1; 13:3; Acts 10:38; 11:21.
127. Byrne, p.27, is of the view that this canticle offers the best summary of the theology of the Gospel. Green, p.111, observes that Mary's canticle is linked with Elizabeth's response, and Zechariah's with those of the angels, shepherds and prophets. Brown, p.379, links Zechariah's blessing with the earlier one of his wife; this scene, like the previous one, moves to termination with a canticle proclaiming what God has done.

128. Green, p.115, notes that the gift of the Spirit was often bestowed for the purpose of prophecy, which provided God's perspective on events.
129. Marshall, p.90.
130. See Brown: introduction 68a; body 68b-77 (subdivided: 68b-71; 72-75; 76-77); conclusion 78-79. The insertion (v.76-77) is probably a Lucan addition to the original hymn. Some (McBride, p.33, Marshall, p.86) consider verses 76-79 to be a birthday hymn in honour of the child (a *genethliakon*). For a list of the OT background, see Brown, Table X111, p.386-389. Fitzmyer, 1:382, speaks of a canticle or hymn of praise; like Brown he sees its origin in a Jewish Christian context, whereas the earlier narrative is from a Baptist source. Maluf, *New Perspectives*, p.49, holds that the passage is more a *prophetic proclamation* than a hymn. He divides the text into 2 sections: 68-75, and 76-79. He maintains that Luke himself composed the passage precisely for the context in which it appears.
131. Psa 41:14; 72:18; 106:48. Maluf, p.60, sees Exod 18:10 and 1 Kings 1:48 as more pertinent.
132. For judgement, see Exod 32:34; for saving, see Gen 21:1; Exod 4:31; Ruth 1:6; Psa 105:4. The NRSV translation (*looked favourably*) loses this nuance.
133. 1:78; 7:16; 19:44; Acts 7:23; 15:14.
134. Marshall, p.90. Fitzmyer, 1:383, writes that Zechariah's words could refer to the past, but the Christological thrust of the first part of the canticle makes one realise that Zechariah is praising God for what He has done in the conception and coming birth of Jesus. Green, p.116, refers to the experience of Sarah, and to the Exodus, the paradigmatic act of deliverance from enemies (see Psa 106). Maluf, p.50, challenges the view that this is a messianic hymn. For him the text moves from a consideration of Israel's past, represented by the fathers of Israel (and father Zechariah), to a prophetic glimpse of Israel's future, represented by the child John, the forerunner of Christ, and prophet to a new generation of Israel at the dawn of the messianic age. The past tenses refer to past events in Israel's past as the primary focus. He concludes,

p.68, that the terms in v.68-75 never go beyond the OT hope; they invoke the story and notion of salvation current in the OT.

135. See Psa 18:3; 1 Sam 2:10; Ezek 29:21. For Maluf, p.50-51, comments that the almost universally accepted view that v.68-75 refer to Christ and his saving mission stems from the interpretation of the *horn of salvation* as messianic, referring to Jesus. He, however, sees these verses as referring to Israel's past, and its traditional understanding of salvation.

136. Brown, *Birth*, p.371. Maluf, p.51-59, claims that this phrase is not an allusion to Jesus; the image of brute strength and aggressive military might hardly fits the messiah of compassion and peace. It is a reference to David and his house, through whom God provided protection and salvation for the people.

137. Maluf, p.61, on the other hand, sees this as referring to salvation brought by God to David and his house later in Israel's history.

138. See this theme in Acts 1:16; 3:18; 4:25; 15:7.

139. See Psa 106:10; 18:18.

140. Gen 22:16-18. See Acts 3:25; Gal 3:6-18. See Johnson, p.46.

141. Fitzmyer, 1:384.

142. See Wis 9:3; Josh 24:14. There are echoes of Exodus here.

143. Green, p.117; Fitzmyer, 1:385; Brown, p.372 (Exod 3:12; Deut 11:13). Maluf, p.65, reminds us that worship was part of the story of Exodus and David, and a feature of the story of Joshua: *Israel worshipped the Lord all the days of Joshua and all the days of the elders...*(Josh 24:29).

144. For Maluf, p.63,66, the salvation-type of Israel's past history (especially the Exodus and David's monarchy) took the form of the destruction of enemies. Now, by contrast, a new form of salvation is envisaged, consisting in forgiveness, reconciliation and peace.

145. Green, p.118. This phrasing recalls Isa 40:3 (Mal 3:1,23) and the Elijah figure spoken of in Mal 4:5; but it also anticipates the Gospel proper. Fitzmyer, 1:385, maintains that *Lord* here refers not to Yahweh, but to Jesus.

146. 3:4; 7:27; 16:16.
147. 3:3; 3:10-14. The phrase is first used in Mark 1:4.
148. 4:18; 5:20,24; 7:48-49; 11:4; 17:4; 23:34; 24:47; Acts 2:38; 5:31; 10:43; 13:38; 26:18.
149. The word is *anatolē*. The shoot of Jesse is found in Isa 11:1; and the star of Jacob in Num 24:17; see Matt 2:2. Fitzmyer, 1:387, prefers *shoot* or *scion* with a messianic meaning. Jesus is the Davidic Scion sent by God.
150. Marshall, p.94; Johnson, p.47; Metzger, p.132; Maluf, p.56,fn18; Fitzmyer, 1:388, favour the manuscript evidence for the future tense; Brown, p.373;Evans, p.187, the past. Fitzmyer refers to the switch from past tenses earlier in the canticle to the eschatological future here.
151. Psa 106:10,14LXX. Green, p.119, notes that *darkness* and *shadow* represent an arena of existence ruled by cosmic forces in opposition to God, a domain into which the light of God's redemptive presence is made to shine by the advent of God's agent, the *Dawn*.
152. Psa 107:9-10; Isa 42:6-7; 9:2; 59:8. Evans, p.188, speaks of an existence marked by wholeness and fullness of life.
153. Green, p.114-115, notes the bringing together of two concepts of salvation in this canticle: social/political and religious.
154. Brown, *Birth*, p.383. He believes that the hymn was composed by Jewish Christians. They would be conversant with the martial language of their forebears; they see salvation as already accomplished through Jesus; they have the Anawim mentality; the christology is Jewish and early; in vocabulary and prophetic spirit there is a link with Luke's Jerusalem community in Acts.
155. Isaac (the child grew up: Gen.21:8), Samson (the child became mature, and the Lord blessed him; and the spirit of the Lord began to go with him: Judg.13:24-25LXX), and Samuel (and the child waxed mighty before the Lord: 1 Sam 2:21,26)
156. Brown, *Birth*, p.376-377.

Journey's End

The Nativity in Luke

During the last six days of Advent we reflected on chapter one of Luke's Gospel: the annunciation to Zechariah and then to Mary; the visitation, with the Magnificat canticle; and finally the birth and naming of the future Baptist, concluding with the Benedictus. The latter forms a second diptych with the story of Jesus' birth and naming. The broad sequence of the two birth narratives is the same: birth, circumcision, naming. But whereas the narrative about John centres on the naming of the child, this second narrative focuses on the birth of Jesus. However, the main point of interest is, in fact, the third angelic annunciation, which is followed by the reactions in the final scene, where the various protagonists or characters (Mary, Joseph, the child, the shepherds & other folk) are brought together.[1]

Luke's narrative is divided into two parts for the Christmas Day liturgy, with one section used for the Mass at Midnight (or the late evening), and the rest for the Dawn Mass. The complete text reads as follows:[2]

> In those days a decree went out from Emperor Augustus that all the world should be registered. This was the first registration and was taken while Quirinius was governor of Syria. All went to their own towns to be registered. Joseph also went from the town of Nazareth in Galilee to Judea, to the city of David called Bethlehem, because he was descended from the house and family of David. He went to be registered with Mary, to whom he was engaged and who was expecting a child. While they were there, the time came for her to deliver her child. And she gave birth to her firstborn son and wrapped him in bands of cloth, and laid him in a manger, because there was no place for them in the inn.

In that region there were shepherds living in the fields, keeping watch over their flock by night. Then an angel of the Lord stood before them, and the glory of the Lord shone around them, and they were terrified. But the angel said to them, *Do not be afraid; for see – I am bringing you good news of great joy for all the people: to you is born this day in the city of David a Saviour, who is the Messiah, the Lord. This will be a sign for you: you will find a child wrapped in bands of cloth and lying in a manger.* And suddenly there was with the angel a multitude of the heavenly host, praising God and saying, *Glory to God in the highest heaven, and on earth peace among those whom he favours!*

When the angels had left them and gone into heaven, the shepherds said to one another, *Let us go now to Bethlehem and see this thing that has taken place, which the Lord has made known to us.* So they went with haste and found Mary and Joseph, and the child lying in the manger. When they saw this, they made known what had been told them about this child; and all who heard it were amazed at what the shepherds told them. But Mary treasured all these words and pondered them in her heart. The shepherds returned, glorifying and praising God for all they had heard and seen, as it had been told them.

After eight days had passed, it was time to circumcise the child; and he was called Jesus, the name given by the angel before he was conceived in the womb.

(Luke 2:1-21)

The Setting (2:1-7)
The Census (1-5)

Luke begins his story with an elaborate setting,[3] that of an imperial census ordered by Augustus (Emperor from 30 or 27BC, to AD 14), and conducted by Quirinius, the Governor of Syria, the main Roman province of the region.

This affects Joseph in that he is obliged to return from Nazareth in Galilee, where he is living, to his ancestral city, Bethlehem.[4] It is while he is there that Mary, who has accompanied him, gives birth to Jesus.

The census, which is mentioned four times, thus makes it possible for Jesus to be born in Bethlehem, the place of promise. But the setting has other purposes. It provides a solemn beginning for the story of Jesus, emphasising the cosmic and universal significance of his birth. His birth is an event which touches the whole world, not simply Israel, as in the case of John. Through his edict, the Emperor is unwittingly serving God's plan, as Cyrus did in the Old Testament; Augustus is subservient to a greater purpose and sovereignty. Later, the new religion inaugurated by Jesus will spread to the confines of the Empire and beyond. Perhaps Luke saw it as significant that Jesus was born in the reign of Augustus, the Emperor who finally brought an era of peace after a century of war (the Pax Romana). He was popularly called the saviour of the world, and accorded honours appropriate for the divine.[5] This statement Luke challenges. It is the child whose birth he is about to describe who brings real peace and is the world's true saviour, as the Benedictus celebrated.

From a historical point of view there are problems with this introduction.[6] There is no other evidence that Augustus ordered a census of his world. He did, however, accumulate a lot of statistics for taxation purposes, possibly as a result of more local provincial censuses. A census was a symbol of Roman overlordship, a reminder that Israel was a conquered people. Quirinius, the Roman legate in Syria, was indeed responsible for a census in Judea, probably for taxation purposes, but that was in AD 6, ten years later, coinciding with the deposing of Archelaus and the annexation of Judea. It did not apply to Galilee.[7] This problem seems to have no definitive conclusion. Scholars tend to take the census as a Lucan literary device to explain the presence of Mary and Joseph in Bethlehem, and consider it to be based on *confused memory*. Nor had the evangelist access to the relevant information available to the contemporary historian.

We are dealing, not with a scientifically determined chronology, but with purposeful storytelling.[8] The Roman system did not demand enrolment in one's ancestral city but one's place of residence.[9] It is not clear why Mary had to go as well, and it is uncertain whether she was required to register. Joseph may have wished to secure her protection, given the nature of her pregnancy, and was afraid to leave her alone at home in Nazareth; he wanted them to be together for the birth.[10]

Luke, according to most manuscripts, uses the term *betrothed*. This is probably intended to suggest that the marriage had not been consummated, though presumably they were now living together. It indicates subtly that Joseph is not the child's father, and links with the earlier narrative. His Davidic descent is emphasised.[11]

The Birth of Jesus (6-7)

The vastness of imperial Rome and the biblical context of the Royal House of David are in strong contrast with the humble event of this child's birth. God reverses normally accepted values, as we saw in the Magnificat.

The time came for her to deliver her child refers both to the gestation period and the angelic announcement, as God's plan unfolds.[12] There is no indication of the length of time spent in Bethlehem prior to the birth of Mary's child, but a period of time is implied. The evangelist simply and soberly states the fact that while they were there, she gave birth to a son. The child is said to be her firstborn, fulfilling the angel's announcement. Some take this to imply that she had other children later, the brothers and sisters referred to during the ministry. But the word firstborn does not demand this. What is important for the evangelist is that Jesus, as the firstborn, must be presented in the Temple and consecrated to God, and that he should receive the position and privileges which tradition gave to the firstborn: the birthright and Davidic inheritance.[13]

Mary performs two actions for the newly born child: she *wrapped him in swaddling clothes* and she *laid him in a manger*. Swaddling consisted in wrapping linen strips like bandages around the child's limbs to ensure that they grow straight, and was a normal expression of parental care. Rather than an indication of poverty and lowliness, as some suggest, the detail is probably intended to recall the description of Solomon's swaddling in the Book of Wisdom,[14] and so is not incompatible with the child's royal Davidic background. The word *phatnē* translated *manger* can refer to an open feeding area, or a trough for feeding cattle, which could be movable or be a cavity shelf in the rock. It can also mean a stall where cattle are tied up. Many scholars see this as an indication of poverty and humility: at his birth, Jesus had to accept the habitation of animals. The detail of the manger probably holds symbolic significance, for it is repeated three times and is referred to as a sign. One suggestion is that it recalls:

The ox knows its owner and the donkey its master's crib; Israel does not know, my people do not understand.(Isaiah 1:3)

This situation is reversed or repealed by the later coming of the shepherds, as Israel begins to find its way back to God, and begins to know the manger of the Lord.[15] Incidentally, there is no specific mention of the animals in Luke; given the situation described, it can be presumed. Their appearance at the crib is a later, long-standing and appropriate development.

Luke makes an explanatory comment that there was no room for them in the *katalyma*. This word is open to a variety of interpretations, and precision is difficult to achieve. Basically, it indicates a place where a traveller lays down his baggage when stopping over whilst on a journey. Its basic meaning is a guest room.[16] Traditionally, it has been taken to be an inn, like a khan or caravansary, where large numbers found shelter under one roof. There were two levels, one for people and one for the animals. The traditional view is that Luke's idea would be that the hostel was full, presumably because of the influx of travellers caused by the census. Maybe because of overcrowding, courtyard space normally kept for the animals was brought into use. So some vague word like living space or lodging is probably best.[17]

Bailey is critical of this traditional view.[18] He notes that Joseph was returning to his village of origin. In the Middle East historical memories are long, and the extended family, with its connection to its village of origin, is important. Joseph could have appeared in the village and told people he was son of Heli, son of Matthat etc, and most homes would have been open to him. He was also from the family of King David, and the village was known locally as the city of David. Being of the Davidic family, Joseph would have been welcome anywhere in town.

In every culture a woman about to give birth is given special attention. Rural communities always assist their women in childbirth regardless of the circumstances. The Bethlehem community would have sensed its responsibility to find adequate shelter and provide the care needed. To turn away a descendant of David in such circumstances would be an unspeakable shame on the village. Mary also had relatives in a nearby village. If Joseph had been unsuccessful in Bethlehem, they would have gone to Zechariah and Elizabeth. Joseph had time to make necessary arrangements. The text does not indicate that the child was born the night they arrived. This myth dates from the Protoevangelium of James, who wasn't a Jew, didn't understand Palestinian geography or Jewish tradition, and wrote 200 years after the birth of Jesus.

In traditional Middle Eastern villages, simple village homes had two rooms. One was for guests; it would be attached to the end of the house or on the roof.[19] The main room was the family room in which the entire family cooked, ate, slept and lived. The end of the room next to the door was either a few feet lower than the rest of the floor or blocked off with heavy timbers. Each night into that designated area the family cow, donkey and a few sheep would be driven. And every morning those same animals were taken out and tied up in the courtyard of the house. The animal stall would then be cleaned for the day. Such homes traced back to the time of David and up to mid-20th century (3000 years). The peasant wants the animals in the house for warmth in winter and because they are safe from theft.

The mangers, perhaps two of them, were dug out of the lower end of the living room. This was sloped in direction of the animal area, which aids sweeping and washing. If a cow is hungry at night, it can stand up and eat from the manger. Mangers for sheep were made of wood and placed on the floor of the lower level.[20]

Current popular tradition demands an inn with a *no vacancies* sign! But the Greek does not refer to a room in an inn; it simply means *space* in the *katalyma*. This is not the ordinary word for a commercial inn, which is *pandocheion*, as in the story of the Good Samaritan, meaning *receive all*. *Katalyma* is simply a place to stay. Later in Luke's Gospel it is a guest room, upstairs, used for the Last Supper.[21] So Luke says that Jesus was placed in a manger in the family room because in that home the guest room was already full.[22]

The Annunciation to the Shepherds (2:8-14)
The Message and Sign (8-12)

The second half of the episode centres on the angelic annunciation to the shepherds. Shepherds were not too highly regarded at the time. They were peasants, poor and marginalised. Rabbinic traditions label them as unclean, possibly because flocks ate private property.[23] In post New Testament times they were on lists of proscribed trades; perhaps such ideas were alive in Jesus' time. They were close to the bottom of the social scale in their society. They had a reputation for petty theft; they were partial to pasturing their sheep on other people's land; they tended to be neglectful of religious observance; they were not permitted to function as legal witnesses.[24] They would therefore be classed amongst the lowly ones, forerunners of the many ordinary folk who will encounter Jesus later during his ministry, the *poor* to whom the Gospel will be preached. From the outset, Jesus is part of their world, and in this way his mission is anticipated. They gather to see the descendant of David, who in the tradition was the shepherd of the flock of Israel; his messianic successor was also to be a shepherd leader.[25] The shepherds are also outside the circle of Jesus' family. The contrast with the emperor and powerful is strong; the Good News comes to poor shepherds, not the rulers or urban elite.

In the narrative, a group of such shepherds are keeping night guard over their sheep in the fields, probably watching in shifts.[26] More importantly, the darkness stands in contrast with the coming light of God's glory, the sign of God's presence.[27] Some scholars note that their being out in the open suggests that winter is over; others point out that the place traditionally associated with the shepherds' fields is below the snowline. Really there is nothing in the narrative to indicate clearly the time of year.

There follows a third angelic annunciation, structured according to the basic pattern, though here it concerns a birth which has already taken place. An angel, probably Gabriel again, stands over the shepherds, and the glory of the Lord shines round about them.[28] The term *glory* usually refers to God's presence in majesty, sometimes considered visible in the form of a bright light.[29] The initial reaction of the shepherds is, as is to be expected, intense terror. The angel bids them to lay aside their fear, substituting it with great joy, which is a feature of chapter one also, as we have seen. He then proceeds to impart joyful news for them and for all the people. Many think that *people* here probably refers only to Israel; others, however, maintain that it is has a universalist meaning.[30] This joyful news[31] is densely expressed:

> Today in the town of David a Saviour has been born
> to you; he is Christ the Lord.

Today can be taken literally, but may also have an eschatological ring: it denotes the long awaited day of salvation, on which are fulfilled the hopes of centuries. Luke frequently emphasises the now of God's deliverance. The term Saviour is rare in the New Testament, and is found only here in the Synoptics. At the time, Gentiles were looking for a saviour, and the term was applied to the Emperor and other Hellenistic rulers, and was used in the mystery cults. The Jewish background, however, is strong: the Jews longed for a king to liberate them from oppression. In the Old Testament it is Yahweh who is the saviour. Luke believes that God is now acting through Jesus in order to save.[32]

The child is given the titles Messiah and Lord, an unusual combination without the article. In the Septuagint, *Lord* is used of Yahweh. Luke uses it frequently of Jesus during the ministry. In Isaiah 9:1-7, the interpretive context, we find the Good News that a child is born to the people, a son given; a list of names or titles follows: wonderful counsellor, everlasting father, prince of peace. For these titles Luke substitutes titles from the Christian kerygma: Saviour, Christ, Lord, titles usually associated with the resurrection.[33] At this stage the full meaning and implications of these titles is not evident.

Without their asking, a normal occurence in annunciation narratives, the shepherds are given a sign. Paradoxically, the child proclaimed in such exalted terms is to be found in extremely lowly conditions. They will recognise him by the swaddling clothes and manger. The discovery will point to the validity of what has been said about his significance for the future of the people.[34]

Bailey notes that initially the shepherds were afraid of the angels. Then, because they were asked to visit the child, they expected to be rejected by the parents if he was the Messiah.[35] The angels tell them that they would find him in an ordinary peasant home like their own, not in a governor's mansion. The manger was a sign for lowly shepherds. They must have found the family in perfectly adequate accommodation; otherwise they would have moved them to their own homes. The honour of the village rested on their shoulders. They obviously felt that they could not offer better hospitality than had already been made available.

The Angels and their Canticle (13-14)

At this point the annunciation pattern is disrupted by the appearance of an immense throng of the heavenly hosts, army or entourage.[36] They sing the praises of God. The Sanctus canticle in Isaiah probably served Luke as an antecedent. Glory in 2:9 referred to the visible manifestation of God's majesty; here it means the honour which angels and men pay to God in recognition of his majesty, transcendence and gracious mercy.[37] On earth, it is the gift of peace which the angels celebrate. Peace here does not mean the cessation of violence, a peace of the kind introduced by Augustus. It means the full sum of blessings associated with the coming of the Messiah, as prophesied by Zechariah; scriptural shalom, which indicates peace with justice and universal healing.[38] In particular, it connotes the healing of man's estrangement from God, the forgiveness of sins, the establishment of a loving relationship between God and mankind, which introduces inner harmony and better human relationships. This promise of peace and wellbeing is offered to those favoured by God, those with whom God is pleased, those on whom God's redemptive mercy has been bestowed. Some understand this as suggesting the universal implications of Jesus' coming, since the Good News is for all people, not just Israel.[39] God's mercy is inclusive; shalom is for the cosmos. Again there is the sense of God's saving freedom and choice. There is an echo of this hymn on the disciples' lips later in the Gospel when Jesus enters the city of Jerusalem: *Peace in heaven and glory in the highest heavens!*[40]

The Reactions (2:15-20)

The reading for the Mass during the night concludes with the excitement engendered by the visit and singing of the angels. As we gather at dawn, the focus is placed on the different responses to what has taken place. There is the initial response of the shepherds to the angels' message, and then a threefold response: from the crowd, from Mary and from the shepherds again.

The Shepherds (15-17)

On the return of the angels to heaven, which brings the annunciation structure to its conclusion, the shepherds express their belief that they have received a revelation from God through the angel, and they respond positively in obedience by going over to Bethlehem with haste, like Mary earlier.[41] The little ones are open and responsive. No details of their search are provided, but there they find Mary and Joseph (in that order, which is significant in that culture) and the cradled child. What was promised is fulfilled. They tell their story to the couple and, as we learn shortly, to others around, informing them of what has happened and what the angel has told them.

The shepherds were made welcome at the manger; the unclean were judged to be clean; the outcasts become honoured guests; the song of the angels was sung to the simplest of all.[42]

Three Further Responses (18-20)

Luke then provides three reactions to the revelation of God's saving mystery in the child: the response of the audience, of Mary, and of the shepherds. The others present at the birthplace, in parallel with the relatives and neighbours in the earlier Baptist story, who hear what the shepherds have to say, react with wonder and astonishment. A similar reaction has occurred at the circumcision and naming of John. Here, however, there is no indication of further interest; amazement is not faith nor a guarantee of real understanding.

Mary, who stands in pivotal position at the centre of this threefold structure, treasures these things and ponders them in her heart, as had Elizabeth's neighbours at John's naming. This phrase about pondering in her heart, which is again applied to Mary in the later episode in the Temple,[43] is an expression found frequently in revelation and apocalyptic contexts in the Old Testament as a response to something mysterious which is beyond human comprehension and control. Mary does not fully understand what God is doing in her life; she reflects in order to grasp the full meaning of it all; she is open to God's action and reflectively awaits the developments of God's purposes in God's time. She alone appears in the later ministry period, where she is presented by Luke as a believer and as a disciple, a form of response which she has already initiated. Things will become clearer only with the coming of the Spirit at Pentecost.[44]

The shepherds leave and return to their flocks, praising and glorifying God, their part in the story completed, rather like the Magi in the Matthaean story. They have linked what they have heard with what they have seen, and have made known to others what was made known to them, thus being in a sense the first evangelists. They represent for Luke the future believers who will likewise praise God for what they have heard and seen, an earthly praise which echoes that of the angels in heaven.

Circumcision and Naming (2:21)

This final significant detail is not included in the liturgical reading.[45] Observing the pattern of events followed in his treatment of the story of John the Baptist, Luke next mentions the circumcision of the child eight days later, which underlines his solidarity with the human situation, and his identification with his people.[46] The evangelist's main emphasis, however, is not on the circumcision, but on the naming of the child in accordance with the command of the angel to Mary. Jesus' name is thus given by God. The obedience of Mary and Joseph to God's word is also illustrated. It comes as a surprise that the meaning of the name Jesus, *Yahweh saves,* is not underlined, in spite of that role being mentioned earlier.

Reflections

A newborn child is a source of wonder and joy, and is also the epitome of human dependency and need. As we gaze at the manger and the swaddled babe, taking in the atmosphere of the place in Bethlehem where earth and heaven meet, we are gently overwhelmed by a God of such bewildering humility and self-giving love. Like Mary, we are confronted with so much to ponder in our hearts, encouraged to reflect about the meaning of it all. We, unlike the youthful mother Mary, centuries later, know in advance what the outcome will be when her child becomes a man. In Domenico Ghirlandaio's nativity in the church of Santa Trinità in Florence, the babe lies in a sarcophagus filled with hay. *The one laid in a manger at his nativity is destined to be laid in a tomb ..., a tomb that will become the gateway to life.*[47] At his final meal with his disciples, Jesus will take a loaf of bread, give thanks to the Father, break it and give it to his disciples, with the words: *This is my body, which is given for you.* And as the disciples subsequently argue as to which of them is the greatest, Jesus says: *I am among you as one who serves.*[48] The humility and self-giving love witnessed in the manger reaches a climax on Calvary's hill.

As we ponder Luke's Christmas scene in gratitude and wonder, we cannot escape the stark invitation to embrace Jesus' servant, self-giving lifestyle which is his revelation of the self-giving servant God.

In almost every section of the Infancy Narrative we have seen how Luke's God turns our human expectations and presuppositions upside down. A God of compassion and faithful love, He is a God of freedom and surprises. The greatest surprise remains the depth of his love for us, his reaching out to draw us into his embrace.

The hillside shepherds in the storyline, on recovering from their initial shock at the angel's message of revelation, make their speedy journey to Bethlehem to find the child. They tell their story to Mary and Joseph and the others who are present. They are bearers of the Good News brought by the angel. Like them, we are called to leave the crib and journey on to make known to others the ongoing daily significance of the Christmas celebration. Our lives are meant to be *Good News* for those we encounter in the wide variety of circumstances of a typical day. We take with us the joy of knowing God's unfathomable love and offer of salvation in Jesus. Another journey begins, the journey into mission.

The Nativity in John

John begins his Gospel with an inspiring, rather poetic piece usually referred to as the Prologue, which Raymond Brown calls *the pearl within the Gospel.*[49] It is possibly an adaptation of an early Christian hymn based on reflection about Wisdom in the Old Testament. This could have originated in Johannine circles. It provides a kind of summary of salvation history. It furnishes us with a key with which to unlock the deepest meaning of the narrative which follows, introducing the central character, the plot and the main themes. It tells about the Word, the Logos, the communicating of God.

Background

This term *Logos* already had a long history, in Greek thought, from the time of Heraclitus in the sixth century BC, who considered the Logos to be the principle of unity and order in the flux and change of the universe. Later, the Stoic philosophers considered the Logos to be the power which shaped and guided the world. It was, however, the Jewish background which seems to have had the determining influence on the evangelist. The biblical concept of the *Word of God* (dabar in Hebrew) is extremely rich.[50] This term (dabar) is used in two ways. Firstly, it has to do with understanding, enlightenment and revelation. In this sense, God manifested his will for the people in the conduct of their lives, the ten *words*, the Law. Through the prophets God enlightened Israel about the events of its history. God's word was also a word of promise and of judgement. A word inevitably entails communication, and so something of God's mystery and identity came to be understood by the people of Israel. Secondly, the word of God is dynamic and creative;[51] it directs the course of history; it is healing, sustaining and life-giving. And God said: *Let there be light.*

The second reading for this third Christmas Mass is apposite:

At various times in the past and in various different ways, God spoke to our ancestors through the prophets; but in our own time, the last days, he has spoken to us through his Son. (Heb 1:1-2)

In the Old Testament presentation of Wisdom there are parallels for almost every detail of the Prologue's description of the Word.[52] Wisdom, in Greek *Sophia*, is said to come from the mouth of God and exists at the beginning before the world was created.[53] Wisdom remains with God, and has a role in creation.[54] Wisdom is light and life for human beings, and sets up her tent amongst them. By some, Wisdom is rejected.[55] The Wisdom literature identified Wisdom and the Law (Torah).[56] The concept of Wisdom has a profound influence on the Prologue, and on the Christology of the whole Gospel. This identification proved crucial in the restructuring of Judaism after the destruction of the Temple; the Pharisees looked to the Torah as the source of access to the divine mysteries, and the Christian community looked to Jesus.[57]

Another influence on John may have come from rabbinical reflection on the Law, which was said to be light and life and the supreme example of God's love. Law (Torah) and the word of God are often interchangeable terms. It is even said to have been created before all things, and as having served as the pattern on which God created the universe.

The Text

In the beginning was the Word, and the Word was with God, and the Word was God. He was in the beginning with God. (1:1-2)

The Prologue commences, like the book of Genesis, in the beginning. But this beginning is beyond the beginning, beyond our time and space categories in the realm of the utterly and unimaginably *Other*: *The Word was with God, and the Word was God. With* can denote *presence with*, or *turned towards* in dynamic communion. The Word in the presence of God is turned in loving, inseparable communion towards God; there was a corresponding turning of

God towards the Word. There is at once profound intimacy and clear distinction.[58] The two are so close that whatever one is, the other is (What God was, the Word was).

The role of the Word in creation is described. The whole of the created universe, every item, came into being through the Word. *In the biblical account of creation, God speaks and things happen; his Word forms the world.*[59] The twin themes of life and light are introduced, and light's opposite, the darkness, and the inevitable conflict between these polarities. Creation through the Word of its nature entails communication and revelation. All created reality is a word from God, it bears God's stamp.

> All things came into being through him, and without him not one thing came into being. What has come into being in him was life, and the life was the light of all people. The light shines in the darkness, and the darkness did not overcome it. (1:3-5)

Light is an image for the presence and enlivening power of God, and darkness symbolises ignorance, unbelief, and sin, which lead to death. In this way the role of the Word in the human situation is broached, as the Word in God becomes the light of the world, the source of a revelation which is life-giving. But where there is light, there is the possibility of darkness. The issue of our human response is introduced, as darkness vainly struggles to comprehend or overpower the light. Some scholars believe that here reference is made to a specific past event in which light and darkness clashed, the Genesis story of the Fall. Others take it as a general reference to the fact that darkness always attempts to extinguish the light, and that this has been a pattern throughout human history.[60] The light continues to shine, nevertheless, because of God's saving promise. A few scholars take it as a subtle reference to the passion and resurrection, the cosmic clash of light and darkness on the cross, and the light's ultimate victory.[61]

The movement of the Prologue accelerates and the texture changes from poetry to prose with the rather abrupt introduction of a historical figure, sent from God, whose name was John. His mission in life is then outlined:

> He came as a witness to testify to the light, so that
> all might believe through him. He himself was not
> the light, but he came to testify to the light. The
> true light, which enlightens everyone, was coming
> into the world. (1:7-9)

His principal role in this Gospel is to be a witness, to testify, to point to another. He is a secondary figure. The genuine light, the world's revealer, stands at the threshold.

Words look for a response. The phrase in the Prologue which speaks of light and darkness, and the fact that the darkness could not overcome the light, is the first suggestion of human response. This is rendered more explicit when we are informed that the world, created and sustained by the Word, did not recognise or welcome the light, and that his own domain and his own people, Israel, did not accept him. In John's Gospel the term *world* is used in three senses: material reality, the theatre of human affairs, the area which is hostile and in the power of evil.

Others, however, responded positively, coming to accept him and to believe in his name; the name means all that a person represents.[62] These, by God's gift, became children of God. They did so, not through physiological process, or as a result of human frailty or conscious human decision, but by God's free gift.[63] The plot of the story is thus revealed, as in the course of the narrative which unfolds, human beings respond to the revelation Jesus brings either by accepting in faith, and are drawn into the life of God, or by remaining closed, thus opting for darkness and death.

That decisive coming of the authentic light of revelation is described in the memorable phrase which juxtaposes two incompatibles: the Word *became flesh and lived amongst us.* The term *Word* is here used again. This is the most profound of paradoxes. That *Word* now enfleshed shares our human experience, our human story, and has a human name, Jesus.[64] In the subsequent narrative of his ministry, he is presented as the light of the world, the Revealer, and as the source of life, as the evangelist carefully develops these Prologue motifs. The term *flesh* denotes humanity in its weakness, finitude, vulnerability, transitoriness, but it does not in John include the aspect of sinfulness which is sometimes found in Paul's writings.

The verb here translated as *lived* really means *pitched his tent.*[65] The tent or tabernacle played a significant role in the unfolding history and life of the people of Israel. Being initially a nomadic group, the tent was obviously a basic commodity, a survival guarantee. It signified home and family and security and belonging. The tent later came to have profound religious significance for the people too. In Exodus 25:8-9, Israel is told to make a tent or tabernacle so that God could dwell amongst his people: *the tabernacle became the site of God's localised presence on earth.*[66] And later, when Israel finally settled in Jerusalem, and life became more sedentary, the Temple which Solomon constructed took over this role and became the religious centre of Israel, the place of God's presence. And this was true also of the Second Temple, which stood proudly, richly embellished by Herod, in Jesus' day. Now, it is Jesus who is the localisation of God's presence, the place where God dwells.[67]

The Christian community behind this hymn and this Gospel narrative claims to have seen God's glory, *we have seen his glory, the glory as of a father's only son,* God's powerful presence in Jesus, the revealer of God's steadfast, enduring and faithful love.[68] From now on the relationship between God and the Logos, with which the Prologue began, will be described in terms of a relationship between Father and Son.

The Prologue closes with four points. The Baptist bears witness which confirms his inferiority to the one coming chronologically after him in birth and ministry, but being before him in status and in pre-existence; he testifies to the absolute primacy of the one following him. The believing community behind the Gospel acknowledges the abundance of God's blessings which they have received in Jesus, the fullness of revelation and truth. The Greek can mean *one blessing on top of another*, a sense of accumulation, a ceaseless stream of gifts; or it can mean *one gift instead of another,* which leads into the following sentence.

The Law is seen as the gift of God which came through Moses; God's gift of the *fullness of truth* and enduring love has come through Jesus. The old is fulfilled, perfected, replaced by the new; some refer to shadow and substance. And we now know that the human name of the enfleshed Word is Jesus. Finally, the uniqueness of the revelation which Jesus brings is emphasised. As Jesus walks among us, he is always at the Father's side in closeness and intimacy, close to the Father's heart; because of that relationship, he is uniquely capable of revealing God.

So now we, the readers, know what the coming story is all about. We know who is behind it all; we have met the main character, Jesus, and we know where he *comes from.* We know the purpose of his coming among us, as light and life, as the one who enables us to become the children of God. We are aware of the plot of the story, as human beings recognise his identity or fail to do so, and respond to him and his revelation by accepting in faith, or by remaining closed, opting for darkness and death. We are challenged about our response.

We have also met themes which will recur throughout the narrative: origins, life, light and darkness, sending, witness, world, knowledge, believing, birth, seeing, glory, truth, revelation, response, replacement. We have privileged insight as we follow the narrative ahead of us; we always know more than the other actors in the drama, and this enables us to catch the irony sometimes. We are already caught up in the drama which is about to unfold.

Reflections

This text from the fourth evangelist encapsulates the meaning and wonder of Christmas in that one paradoxical sentence: *the Word became flesh and pitched tent in our midst.* Admittedly there is no Bethlehem, no mention of Mary or Joseph or the shepherds or the angels or manger or swaddling clothes. But what Matthew and Luke proclaim in dramatic narrative, the Prologue proclaims in a succinct sentence. Through this human being who came to be known as Jesus, God is present in our world in a unique way. The deeds and words of Jesus are the words and deeds of God.[69]

Early in John's presentation of the ministry of Jesus he is approached by Nicodemus, a pre-eminent teacher in Israel. After explaining that for entry into the *Kingdom of God*, it is necessary to be born of water and Spirit, Jesus moves on to make a statement which sums up the Gospel in a nutshell:

> For God so loved the world that he gave his only Son, so that everyone who believes in him may not perish but may have eternal life. (3:16)

The enfleshment of the *Word* is the gift of God, the expression of the outpouring of God's love for our world and our salvation. And this salvation consists in having eternal life, which for the fourth evangelist means our sharing in the life of God now in the present, and later beyond the grave. In giving us his Son, God gives us all he has to give; God keeps nothing back. Through pitching tent in our midst, the *Word* comes to share our human life experience so that we may share in the life of the God who sent him. Jesus makes the Father known; he reveals to us the depths of the Father's love. The highpoint and climax of this revelation happens on Calvary when the Son is *lifted up*. On the cross, through his laying down his life in self-gift, he makes known the glory of God; that is, he discloses the life-giving and loving nature of God, and this exceeds our wildest dreams. It is this mystery of love which embraces us at Christmas, and which we celebrate with joy and gratitude.

The mystery, of course, endures beyond Christmas. God's overspilling love inundates our world unceasingly. The Word continues to pitch his tent, this time in the heart of each one of us. He abides permanently in the innermost depth of our being; there he has made his home; he is nearer to us than we are to ourselves.[70] He is with us, with us in our uniqueness and originality; he cares for us as if we were the only one he has to care for, as St Augustine puts it.[71] Perhaps the invitation and challenge of Christmas is to allow ourselves to become aware of that presence and love, to become aware of who we really are at the core of our identity. Such awareness is transforming and life-giving; it emerges through stillness and silent prayer; it begins to colour everything we do. Nothing is ordinary any more.

Having accomplished our Advent journey, and celebrated God's Christmas love, perhaps the next journey on which we may wish to embark or re-engage more seriously is this journey into stillness, silence, and contemplative prayer. It is a journey which more and more people are taking up and finding attractive and compelling. It is a journey which leads us more deeply into the mystery of the God of Love.

Endnotes

1. For details see Brown, *Birth*, p.408-412.
2. Brown, *Adult*, p.15, notes that nothing that happens in this second chapter of Luke presupposes what happens in the first; it was probably originally independent. The focus in Matthew 2 and Luke 2 is the divine proclamation to an audience (the Magi and the shepherds).
3. The structure which I am following is that of Brown, *Birth*, p.410.
4. Marshall, p.105, suggests that Joseph may have had property in Bethlehem; also Evans, p.196. Fitzmyer, 1:405, maintains that there is no hint of this. The census recalls that instigated by David (2 Sam 24:1-9). See also Psa 87:6.
5. On the imperial cult, see Green, p.122-123; also Brown, *Adult*, p.18. The Myrian inscription reads: *divine Augustus Caesar, son of a god...saviour of the whole world.*
6. Brown, *Adult*, p.17 says *formidable historical difficulties*. For a full discussion see Marshall, p.99-104; Fitzmyer, 1:399-405. Johnson, p.49, states that Luke simply has the facts wrong.
7. For a detailed discussion of issues connected with the census, see Brown, *Birth*, p. 413-418, and Appendix VII, p.547-555.
8. Johnson, p.51-52; see Fitzmyer, 1:393.
9. The terminology used, *going up*, and *city of David*, normally refers to Jerusalem.
10. Bailey, *Jesus through Middle Eastern Eyes* (London, SPCK 2008), p.46. Borg & Crossan, p.147-148, maintain that the Roman system focused on where a person lived; Mary would not have been obliged to register. Also McBride, p.36.
11. Note the links with Gabriel's earlier message (1:27, 32-33) and Mic 5:2. Fitzmyer, 1:406, asserts that Luke knows of no Davidic connection for Mary.

12. Green, p.128. King, *New Perspectives*, p.74-75, makes some interesting comments on Luke's subtle use of indicators of time; usually, God's time is also involved.

13. Johnson, p.50; Marshall, p.106; Green, p.128; Evans, p.199; Fitzmyer, 1:408; Brown, *Birth*, p.398. See Exod 4:22-23; 13:2,12; 34:19; Num 3:12-13; Deut 21: 15-17; Jer 31:9.

14. Wis 7:4-5: *nursed with care in swaddling clothes.*

15. Green, p.136: the sign *lays bare God's gracious act to embrace anew, through this child, his people.* See Brown, *Adult*, p.20. Johnson, p.53, wonders whether the three details: wrapped... placed...no place, perhaps anticipate the threefold rhythm of the burial scene (23:53). See also Green, p.124. I. Boxall, *Luke's Nativity Story* in *New Perspectives*, p.33-34, upholds the link between cradle and grave; he also sees a link between the angelic annunciation of Christ's birth to the shepherds, and the proclamation of the resurrection to the women at the tomb (p.32).

16. Green, p.128; Brown, *Birth*, p.399-401. Borg & Crossan, p.150, suggest a caravansary: an open courtyard surrounded with doorless, covered rooms; the rooms were all gone, so Jesus is born among the animals in the courtyard, and laid in a feeding trough. Likewise Byrne, p.31. Fitzmyer, 1:408, too opts for a public caravansary where groups of travellers would spend the night under one roof.

17. King, *New Perspectives*, p.67-69, defends the traditional view, preferring to translate the term as *inn*. He sees this in the wider context of Luke-Acts as a whole, in which no human agency or setback is going to thwart the divine project. Johnson, p.52, sees Mary and Joseph as *transients*, like the homeless of our contemporary cities. There are echoes of the Samuel story: 1 Sam 1:18.

18. Bailey, p.25-37.

19. See 1 Kings 17:19 concerning Elijah.

20. See 1 Sam 28:24; Jud 11:29-40; Matt 5:14-15; Luke 13:10-17. Bailey, p.31, quotes W Thompson from 1871: birth took place in an ordinary house of some common peasant, and the baby was laid in one of the mangers; also E.F.F. Bishop before 1950. For more than 100 years scholars resident in

the Middle East have understood Luke 2:7 as referring to a family room with mangers cut into the floor at one end. Green, p.128-9 concurs; he comments that there was probably no commercial inn in Bethlehem, since it stood on no major roads. Marshall, p.107, too suggests a room in a private house.

21. 22:10-12. The verbal form (*kataluein*) is used in 9:12 and 19:7, meaning to find lodging, or be a guest.

22. The word is used in 2 Sam 7:6LXX as the dwelling place of God's presence during the journey in the desert. In 1 Sam 1:18, it is used of the place where Hannah and her husband stay at Shiloh. See also Jer 14:8.

23. Bailey, p.35; Brown, *Birth*, p.420-424; Caird, p.61; Green, p.130, speaks of peasants, located toward the bottom of the scale of power and privilege.

24. McBride, p.40, observes that shepherds may have had a place of importance in the folklore of the Israelite people, but had no place of importance in their society at the time of Jesus.

25. 1 Sam 16:11; 17:15; 2 Sam 5:2; Jer 3:5; Ezek 34:11-12; Mic 5:4. Brown, *Birth*, p.421-424, believes that a midrashic reflection on Mic 5:1 and Gen 35:21 underlies Luke's narrative; Fitzmyer, 1:396, disputes this; he maintains (p.395) that the shepherds are introduced because of the association of Jesus' birth with the town of David.

26. Wisdom 18:14-15 may have suggested the choice of night-time by Luke: *When all things were in quiet silence, and the night in its course was half spent, Your all powerful word leaped down from heaven's royal throne.*

27. Green, p.132; the closing line of Zechariah's canticle is recalled.

28. Green, p.131, notes that God's glory is normally associated with the Jerusalem temple, not a farm. Luke is (proleptically) suggesting the coming of a new world.

29. See Exod 13:21; 16:10; 24:17; Ezek 43:2.

30. Johnson, p.50, believes that *people* refers only to Israel. Green, p.133-4, compares it with the universalist references concerning Augustus, claims now being countered.

Marshall, p.109, considers a wider reference possible. Borg & Crossan, p.153-161, discuss *saviour*, *Lord* and *peace* as counter propaganda. Not all would agree.

31. As well as in Isaiah, especially chapters 40-66, the term was used in the pagan world. Green, p.123, notes that this sets Jesus in opposition to the emperor. Also Borg & Crossan, p.158-167, concerning *good news* and *peace*. Byrne, p.33, discounts any hostility to Rome in this.

32. *Saviour* is used of God in 1:47; in 1:69 Jesus is designated *horn of salvation*. See also 2:30.

33. See Isa 52:7; 61:1; Brown, *Birth*, p.425. In Luke 2:9 *Lord* refers to God; in 2:11 to Jesus (as in 1:38 and 1:43). Acts 2:36 reads: *Therefore let the entire house of Israel know with certainty that God has made him both Lord and Messiah*. See Phil 3:20. For Fitzmyer, 1:397, *Messiah* and *Lord* are early kerygmatic titles, stemming from the Jewish Christian community in Palestine. Most scholars prefer the manuscript reading: *Christ the Lord*.

34. Boxall, *New Perspectives*, p.35, sees the shepherds as being commissioned like Moses (Exod 3) and Gideon (Judg 6); they become bearers of the Gospel. He also sees a parallel between 2:20 and 24:52-53.

35. Bailey, p.35-36.

36. See 2 Chr 33:3; Neh 9:6; Jer 8:2. Green, p.131, notes that it is a farm not the temple which is the locus of God's presence; a radically new world is beginning.

37. Brown, *Birth*, p.403.

38. Marshall, p.112; Green, p.137; Evans, p.207. Fitzmyer, 1:411, maintains that the correct translation reads: *Glory in highest heaven to God; and on earth peace for people whom he favours*. It does not mean *men of good will*. Thus our liturgical *Gloria* at Mass is an incorrect translation. In 1:397, he maintains that this hymn is a Lucan composition. Brown, *Birth*, p.403-405, is similar; also NRSV, New Jerusalem Bible.

39. Green, p.131, 137; Borg & Crossan, p.158.

40. 19:38. Some note that in contemporary Jewish literature are to be found hymns of praise for creation. And the Qumran community composed hymns for angels to sing. They also

evinced a sense of being chosen and favoured by God. Brown, *Birth*, p.427, suggests that the canticle could feasibly have been composed by a community of Jewish Christian *anawim*. Borg & Crossan, p.166 note that Roman peace is peace through victory, the peace of Jesus comes through justice.

41. 1:39. The angel speaks of *the city of David*; the shepherds of *Bethlehem* (rather than Jerusalem).

42. Bailey, p.37.

43. 2:51. The verb means to throw together, discuss, debate. See Gen 37:11; Dan 7:28; 8:26; 12:4,9; see also the sapiential tradition: Prov 3:1; Psa 119:11; Sir 39:1-3. King, *New Perspectives*, p.76, translates the verb as *watching*.

44. See Acts 1:14; 2:36.

45. Green, p.140, and Fitzmyer, 1:418, include the circumcision with the following episode, the presentation of the child Jesus in the temple; the parallelism with the Baptist is better preserved in this way. Brown, *Birth*, p.407, includes it here.

46. Gal 4:4; Heb 2:17.

47. Boxall, *New Perspectives*, p.24.

48. Luke 22:19,27.

49. R.E. Brown, *John*, 1:18.

50. A word is a means of a person's self-expression; the basic force of *the Word* is God's self-expression. (See Lincoln, p.95).

51. Psa 33:6; Wis 9:1.

52. See Brown, *John*, 1:521-523; Dodd, p.274-277; Lee, *Flesh and Glory*, p.32; Lincoln, p.98. Wis 9:1-2 links God's Word and God's Wisdom closely: *who have made all things by your word, and by your wisdom have formed humanity.*

53. Sir 24:3; Wis 9:1-2.

54. Sir 1:1; Wis 9:9; Prov 8:27-30.

55. Eccles 2:13; Prov 4:18, 8:35; Sir 24:8-12; Prov 8:31; Sir 15:7; Bar 3:2.

56. Sir 24:8,11,23; Bar 3:36-4:1.

57. Coloe, *God Dwells*, p.20-21.

58. Moloney, *John*, p.35. Coloe, *God Dwells*, p.26, notes that the careful use of articles in 1:1a,b, and the placing of *theos* before the verb *to be* without the article, indicates oneness in nature, not identity in being.

59. Koester, *The Word of Life*, p.30.

60. Brown, *John* 1:26-27, for example, prefers the former option, Barrett, p.134, the latter.

61. Thus Lindars, p.87; Moloney, *Love*, p.12, suggests that a Johannine theology of the cross already begins to appear.

62. Lincoln, p.100-103, defines belief as *a person's total allegiance and wholehearted trust*. He sees the two responses mentioned here as a preview of the Gospel: 1:19-12:50 shows a predominantly hostile response from the nation's leaders, 13:1-17:26 sees Jesus with *his own*.

63. See 3:3-8

64. Lincoln, p.104, states that God's self-communication became embodied.

65. The Greek is *eskēnōsen*.

66. Brown, *John* 1:32.

67. Lincoln, p.104, notes that we find here a fulfilment-and-replacement theme that is developed throughout the narrative.

68. *Full of grace and truth* echoes Exod 33:12-34:9: *a God merciful and gracious, slow to anger, abounding in steadfast love and faithfulness.*

69. Barrett, p.156.

70. John 14:20; 15:4. On the theme of Abiding, see Winstanley, *Symbols*, p.134-147; O'Rourke, p.19, 96.

71. Confessions 3:11.

Bibliography

MATTHEW

Albright W F and Mann C S, *Matthew* (New York, Doubleday 1971)

Beare F W, *The Gospel according to Matthew* (Oxford, Blackwell 1981)

Byrne B, *Lifting the Burden* (Collegeville, Liturgical Press 2004)

Cabrido J A, *The Shepherd of Israel for All Nations A Portrayal of Jesus in the Gospel of Matthew: a Narrative-Critical and Theological Study*, (S T D diss, Pontifical Gregorian University, 2008)

Davis W D and Allison D C, *A Critical and Exegetical Commentary on the Gospel according to Saint Matthew* (London, T&T Clark 2004)

Green H B, *The Gospel according to Matthew* (London, OUP 1975)

Gundry R H, *Matthew* (Grand Rapids, Eerdmans 1982)

Hagner D A, *Matthew*, 2 vols (Nashville, Nelson 2000)

Harrington D J, *The Gospel of Matthew* (Collegeville, Liturgical Press 1991)

Keener C S, *A Commentary on the Gospel of Matthew* (Grand Rapids, Eerdmans 1999)

Luz U, *The Theology of the Gospel of Matthew* (Cambridge, CUP 1995)

McKenna M, *Matthew the Book of Mercy* (New York, New City Press 2007)

Meier J P, *Matthew* (Dublin, Veritas 1980)

Minear P S, *Matthew*, The Teacher's Gospel (London, DLT 1982)

Moloney F J, *This is the Gospel of the Lord* (Year A) (Homebush, St Paul 1992)

Schweizer E, *The Good News according to Matthew* (London, SPCK 1976)

Senior D, *Matthew* (Nashville, Abingdon Press 1998)

Wright N T, *Matthew for Everyone*, 2 vols (London, SPCK 2002)

LUKE

Byrne B, *The Hospitality of God* (Collegeville, Liturgical Press 2000)

Caird G C, *St. Luke* (London, Pelican 1963)

Ellis E E, *The Gospel of Luke* (London, Oliphants 1974)

Evans C F, *Saint Luke* (London, SCM 1990)

Fitzmyer J A, *The Gospel according to Luke* (New York, Doubleday, vol 1 1981, vol 2 1985)

Green J B, *The Gospel of Luke* (Eerdmans, Grand Rapids 1999)

Johnson L T, *The Gospel of Luke* (Collegeville, Liturgical Press 1991)

Fallon M, *Gospel according to St Luke* (Bangalore, Asian Trading Corporation 1997)

Marshall I H, *The Gospel of Luke* (Exeter, Paternoster Press 1978)

Mosetto F, *Lettura del Vangelo secondo Luca* (Rome, LAS 2003)

McBride D, *The Gospel of Luke* (Dublin, Dominican Publications 1991)

Thompson G H P, *The Gospel according to Luke* (Oxford, Clarendon 1972)

Wright N T, *Luke for Everyone* (London, SPCK 2001)

JOHN

Barrett C K, *The Gospel according to John* (London, SPCK 1978)

Brodie T L, *The Gospel according to John* (Oxford, OUP 1993)

Brown R E, *The Gospel according to John* 2 vols (London, Chapmans 1972)

Carter W, *John* (Peabody, Hendrickson 2006)

Chennattu R M, *Johannine Discipleship as a Covenant Relationship* (Peabody, Hendrickson 2006)

Coloe M L, *God Dwells With Us* (Collegeville, Liturgical Press 2001); *Dwelling in the Household of God* (Collegeville, Liturgical Press 2007)

de la Potterie I, *The Hour of Jesus* (Slough, St Paul Publications 1989)

Dodd C H, *The Interpretation of the Fourth Gospel* (Cambridge, CUP 1968)

Koester C R, *Symbolism in the Fourth Gospel* (Minneapolis, Fortress 2003); *The Word of Life* (Grand Rapids, Eerdmans 2008)

Kysar R, *John's Story of Jesus* (Philadelphia, Fortress 1984); *The Maverick Gospel* (Louisville, John Knox Press 2007)

Lee D A, *The Symbolic Narratives of the Fourth Gospel* (Sheffield, JSOT 1994); *Flesh and Glory* (New York, Crossroad 2002)

Lightfoot R H, *St John's Gospel* (Oxford, OUP 1956)

Lincoln A T, *The Gospel according to Saint John*, (London, Baker Academic 2013)

Lindars B, *The Gospel of John* (London, Oliphants 1972)

Moloney F J, *The Gospel of John* (Collegeville, Liturgical Press 1998); *The Gospel of John, Text and Context* (Boston, Brill 2005); *Love in the Gospel of John* (Grand Rapids, Baker Academic 2013)

Schnackenburg R, *The Gospel of John* (London, B&O vol.1 1968, vol. 2 1980, vol.3 1982)

Schneiders S M, *Written That You May Believe* (New York, Crossroad 1999)

Stibbe M W G, *John. Readings* (Sheffield, JSOT Press 1993)

OTHER

Bauckham R, *Jesus and the Eyewitnesses* (Grand Rapids, Eerdmans 2006)

Boring M E, *Mark* (Louisville, Westminster John Knox Press 2006)

Brown R E, *An Adult Christ at Christmas* (Collegeville, Liturgical Press 1978); *A Coming Christ in Advent* (Collegeville, Liturgical Press 1988; *The Birth of the Messiah* (London, Doubleday 1993); *An Introduction to the New Testament* (New York, Doubleday 1997)

Borg M J & Crossan J D, *The First Christmas* (HarperCollins, New York 2007)

Corley J [Ed], *New Perspectives on the Nativity* (London, T&T Clark 2009)

Cunningham M J, *A Connected Life* (Bolton, Don Bosco Publications 2014).

Donahue J R & Harrington D, *The Gospel of Mark* (Collegeville, Liturgical Press 2002)

Dunn J D G, *Jesus Remembered* (Cambridge, Eerdmans 2003); *A New Perspective*, (London, SPCK 2005)

Jalics F, *The Contemplative Way* (New York, Paulist 2011)

Laird M, *Into the Silent Land* (London, DLT 2006); *A Sunlit Absence: Silence, Awareness, Contemplation* (New York, OUP 2011)

McIver R K, *Memory, Jesus and the Synoptic Gospels* (Resources for Biblical Study 59; Atlanta, SBL 2011)

Meier J P, *A Marginal Jew*, 3 vols (Doubleday, New York 1994)

Moloney F J, *Beginning the Good News* (Homebush, St Paul Publications 1992); *The Living Voice of the Gospel* (Dublin, Veritas 2006)

O'Malley D, *Christian Leadership* (Bolton, Don Bosco Publications 2007)

O'Rourke B, *Finding Your Hidden Treasure* (London, DLT 2011)

Powell M A, *What is Narrative Criticism?* (Minneapolis, Fortress 1990)

Ressaguie J L, *Narrative Criticism of the New Testament. An Introduction* (Grand Rapids, Baker Academic 2005)

Rhoads D and Michie D, *Mark as Story* (Philadelphia, Fortress 1982)

The Catholic Bishops' Conference of England and Wales, *The Gift of Scripture*, (London, CTS 2005)

Voorwinde S, *Jesus' Emotions in the Gospels* (London, T&T Clark 2011),

Winstanley M T, *Symbols and Spirituality* (Bolton, Don Bosco Publications 2008); *Lenten Sundays* (Bolton, Don Bosco Publications 2011); *Jesus and the Little People* (Don Bosco Publications 2012)

Don Bosco Publications

Books by Michael T Winstanley SDB

SYMBOLS and SPIRITUALITY

LENTEN SUNDAYS

DON BOSCO'S GOSPEL WAY

JESUS AND THE LITTLE PEOPLE

Children's Books by Kathleen Pearce

KATIE COMES TO MASS

ROSIE GOES TO CHURCH BOOK and DVD

CHLOE AND JACK VISIT THE VATICAN

GOOD NEWS IN THE FAMILY

OUR COLOURFUL CHURCH YEAR

101 SAINTS & SPECIAL PEOPLE

Books by Other Authors

SERVING THE YOUNG by James Gallagher SDB

STARTING AGAIN FROM DON BOSCO by Ian Murdoch SDB

SEAN DEVEREUX by Michael Delmer SDB

GOD OF MANY FACES by Sister Margaret Renshaw FMA

MAMMA MARGARET by Teresio Bosco SDB

BLESSED IS SHE WHO BELIEVED by J J Bartolomé SDB

TEACHER, TEACH US TO PRAY by Sister Winifred Acred FMA

THE WITNESSES by Sister Winifred Acred FMA

MOVING ON by Margaret J Cooke

DON BOSCO - THE PRIEST, THE MAN, THE TIMES by W R Ainsworth

DON'T ORGANISE MY TEARS by Tony Bailey SDB

BOSCO Z BOOK Illustrated Life of Don Bosco for Children

Don Bosco Publications www.don-bosco-publications.co.uk
Books by David O'Malley SDB
SWATCH & PRAY
ADVENT & CHRISTMAS SWATCH
SWATCH JOURNEY THROUGH LENT (with Tonino Passarello)
THE CHRISTIAN TEACHER
CHRISTIAN LEADERSHIP
SCHOOL ETHOS & CHAPLAINCY
WALKING WITH DON BOSCO
PRAYERS TO START MY DAY
PRAYERS TO CLOSE MY DAY
ORDINARY WAYS
A SALESIAN WAY OF LIFE
Books by Michael J Cunningham SDB
TREASURE WITHIN
LET YOUR HEART PRAY
LOST AND FOUND
A TIME FOR COMPASSION
WITHIN & WITHOUT
SALESIANS – CONTEMPLATIVES IN ACTION
A CONNECTED LIFE

DON BOSCO PUBLICATIONS
THORNLEIGH HOUSE
SHARPLES PARK BOLTON, BL1 6PQ
Tel: 01204 308811   Fax 01204 306868
Email sarah@salesians.org.uk
REDUCTIONS AVAILABLE FOR BOOKSHOPS,
CHURCH REPOSITORIES & MULTIPLE COPIES.